SCRIPTURE • FOR • LIVING

Can I Be a Christian on My Own?

Other titles in the
Scripture for Living series

How Can I Pray?
IAN PETIT OSB

Which Way Do I Choose?
PATRICK PURNELL SJ

Why Can't We Stay as We Are?
ANTHEA DOVE

Can I Be a Christian on My Own?

Michael Paul Gallagher SJ
and
Donal Neary SJ

DARTON, LONGMAN AND TODD
LONDON

First published in 1991 by
Darton, Longman and Todd Ltd
89 Lillie Road, London SW6 1UD

ISBN 0-232-51955-2

A catalogue record for this book is available
from the British Library

Phototypeset in 10/12 pt Trump by Intype, London
Printed and bound in Great Britain by
Courier International Ltd, East Kilbride, Scotland

Contents

Introduction

THE WRITINGS OF THE BIBLE – the Scriptures – are the Word of God. They are of supreme importance to all Christians and to all who wish to know and understand the meaning of Christianity. The Bible should be in every Christian home. Every aspect of Christian life and worship should reflect in some way what God says to his people. Catholics have not always been very good at reading and studying the Bible. In 1965 during the Second Vatican Council a document on Scripture as the Word of God (*Dei Verbum*) was published. This has had a marked effect in laying the foundations for an official programme of encouragement to Catholics to make the Bible central to their lives.

Much has happened since then. Every public act of worship has its readings from Scripture. Scripture (both Old and New Testaments) has a significant place in all religious education programmes, whether for adults or for children. The lectionary for the readings at daily and Sunday Mass covers a large amount of Scripture during its three-year cycle. Familiar acts of devotion like the Rosary and the Stations of the Cross have become far more scripturally based.

The positive value of this is obvious enough. But it has also meant that many Catholics have been thrown in at the deep end. They are a little like the Ethiopian in his carriage on the way home from Jerusalem who was reading some Scripture. Philip the Deacon heard him and asked him if he understood what he was reading. 'How can I', the man said, 'unless I have someone to guide me?' (Acts 8:26–40). Most of us do need help if we are to understand what we are reading. It is not that the language of Scripture is particularly difficult; it is rather that its context is so often unfamiliar.

I warmly welcome this series of *Scripture for Living*. Its particular value is that it helps us to see how Scripture is relevant to our daily lives. There are many other books for scholars. This series is for ordinary Christians who treasure Scripture, know for certain that it is of fundamental importance, but who are not sure how to make sense of what they read or how to relate it to their daily lives and experiences.

The pattern of the series is story, bible passage, commentary, reflection and prayer. There is a natural progression in this. The writings in the Bible (which form a whole library really) are about people trying to recognise God in their lives. So the context is just everyday life – the stuff of story. Story leads on naturally to Scripture because Scripture is itself about life in all its variety. So it speaks of love and hate, success and failure, death and resurrection; almost every imaginable human failing and strength finds place in it, simply because it is about real people. The commentary is an aid to understanding. Then, since the ultimate purpose of Scripture is to lead people closer to God, the text finishes with a prayer which ties together what has gone before and shows how our daily lives can be enriched.

The series is ideal for use in groups as well as by individuals. I wish it every success.

+ David Konstant
Bishop of Leeds

Preface

OUR TITLE POSES A QUESTION: Can I be a Christian on my own? The answer given by this book will be 'no', especially not in the context of a vibrant and developing Christian life. Or perhaps a better answer is 'No, but . . .'. You cannot be a Christian totally on your own.

In other words, this book highlights the need for community, for companionship with others in the adventure of being a Christian. We will face questions that many people today have about their relationship with the Church. We will start from stories and experiences, seeking to discover there the roots of our human need for others on any road of growth. Above all we will look at the Scriptures to shed light on this theme of faith not being a solitary journey.

And yet . . . our answer must not become exaggerated. There is another truth, one that is complementary and crucial. Each person is also alone. There is always the need for solitude. Faith speaks and expands in the depths of each heart. To follow Christ is a personal decision. Therefore, an essential strand in becoming a Christian – and one that is a slow and life-long business – involves being 'on my own'.

So our emphasis on community and on Church must not ignore the personal, just as any emphasis on the personal in religion must not ignore the communal. In fact, if religion becomes too privatised, it becomes impersonal. The communal approach must not deny the central mystery of the self, just as a personal approach must not deny the mystery of God in the other.

Perhaps in today's world we are pushed too much towards isolation and individualism, or else towards false collectivity, towards being together only in a superficial way. Christian faith invites us to go beyond both of these unsatisfying forms of life, into a dialogue of true individuality and true community, where one nourishes the other, or is meant to. While the side of the personal is also kept in mind, this book focuses mainly on one side of that dialogue – the need for Christian community.

MICHAEL PAUL GALLAGHER SJ
DONAL NEARY SJ

The Limits of Loneliness

GOING TO UNIVERSITY was such a shock, a much greater one than Gerry expected. For one thing, it was the first time in his life that he had lived away from home. It was also the first time that he had been away from the countryside and his village.

He had known in advance that it would be difficult and that he would miss his family and friends. The university city was a bit too far away to think of going home every weekend but he had planned to see them all at least once a month. In his parents' eyes all would be well because he was going to stay with his aunt, his father's widowed sister, who lived near the university and always took a few students as lodgers.

A home from home? That's not the way it turned out for Gerry in the first month. Right from the start they seemed to rub one another the wrong way. The moment he arrived in the house, she criticised his moustache and then – almost as revenge – he said he didn't like the fish she served up the first evening and left it on the plate.

But the tensions of living-with-auntie were minor in comparison with the trauma of university. Gerry had worked hard for this; for several years it had been his dream to study zoology and he had great expectations about a new social life as well. But here there was nobody to talk to. Everyone else in the class seemed to know a few people and to stick with them. In the whole university there was only one other student from his class at school and she was doing languages so he didn't see her. The shock was simply that nobody seemed to pay any attention to him or to want to get to know him. And in spite of his efforts to join a few clubs, the first month was a very lonely time.

The pain of it hit him one day in the student restaurant. He was sitting with his meal and his newspaper; the paper was his shield against the world. By reading it, he gave the message that being on his own didn't matter. But he wasn't reading it. He was staring at the print and hearing everyone around him having animated conversations. He decided he would write a poem called *Eating on my Ownsomeness*. He liked the title at least. So sitting there in the student cafeteria, he began to write:

> Sole, lone, cut-off, in silent space . . .
> How many words are there
> to say the same reality of stark loneliness?
> I need, I want, I lack, I long
> for others just to know
> that I cannot live
> without being known by them.
> I can go on eating behind a newspaper,
> pretending even to myself
> that this hard-man game is fine
> that I don't hurt or hope.
> But I was made for more
> and the pangs will sting
> until friends arrive to bring
> me from existing into living
> from sulking surviving into blossoming
> and from being lost into being found.

The French philosopher, Descartes, had the famous theory, *Cogito, ergo sum* – I think, therefore I am. But somebody has pointed out that there is a basic flaw in his logic, and that it should read *Cogito, ergo sumus* – I think, therefore *we* are. The point of the correction is simply this: nobody grows alone. Only through others do we become truly human. We first enter into using a language by hearing others speaking it, and most of what we learn we learn through relationships. So Descartes' statement needs that little change of one syllable if it is not to forget the essentially social nature of us all.

The title of this book asks, 'Can I be a Christian on my own?', and the simplest answer is, 'You cannot even be a real person on your own'. We are linked with one another in all sorts of ways, and this is part of being human. It is also part of being Christian.

In Gerry's story, what is important is that he came to a point of recognising this fundamental need. His very loneliness forced him to see that it was unnatural to try to 'survive' as a 'hard man', and that, however it was to happen, he was going to need others in his life. He *had* others in his life but they were far away, and it was their absence that increased his emptiness. Think of the contrast between his image of 'eating behind a newspaper' and the happiness of waking up to friendship that he expresses as the hope of 'being found'. Is it an accident that the last line of his little poem echoes the last phrase of one of the most famous of the parables of Jesus, the story of the Prodigal Son?

. . . *'There was a man who had two sons. The younger one said to his father, "Father, let me have the share of the estate that will come to me." So the father divided the property between them. A few days later, the younger son got together everything he had and left for a distant country where he squandered his money on a life of debauchery.*

'When he had spent it all, that country experienced a severe famine, and now he began to feel the pinch; so he hired himself out to one of the local inhabitants who put him on his farm to feed the pigs. And he would willingly have filled himself with the husks the pigs were

eating but no one would let him have them. Then he came to his senses and said, "How many of my father's hired men have all the food they want and more, and here am I dying of hunger! I will leave this place and go to my father . . . '

(Luke 15:11–18)

In both situations a young man finds himself at his lowest point of emptiness over a question of eating. The Prodigal Son has nothing to eat, except perhaps what is intended for the pigs. Gerry had his meal but somehow his loneliness was magnified by the fact that he felt no contact with those eating around him. Interestingly, in both situations the low point becomes a turning point. Both young men awaken through pain to hope. Each in his own way realises that he is 'made for more', as Gerry's poem puts it.

Perhaps most important of all, each of them discovers a way back to relationship. With Gerry it is only a recognition of a need, but he is so clear about how essential friends are for his humanity that he now has the will to seek them out in a new way. His poem itself is a way of getting in touch with his heart. It is a way of getting his desire into focus. It is a door to change. So too with the young man of the parable. He touches hope, desire, need and sets out on a journey of return to relationship, a journey home.

Leaving aside all the details of this most famous of Jesus' parables, we can pause at the moment in the pigsty. It is a summary of all emptiness, all loneliness of a crippling kind. But it is also a summary of moments of awakening, even through pain. This is often true in people's experience. It is when I seem to hit rock-bottom that I realise it cannot go on, that there are other roads for me. And more often than not these other roads involve some reaching out, making some entry into relationship again.

In this light, it is fascinating that at the beginning of the Bible we find a poetic story of human companionship. 'It is not good that the man should be alone. I will make him a helpmate' (Genesis 2:18). No doubt some remaining details seem a little strange to us nowadays – such as the woman coming from the rib of the man. But this ancient text (probably three thousand years old) captures something beautiful about a deep human need: we are made for one another, not for walking through life alone. The companionship will take many forms – the commitment of marriage; the fidelity of friends; the ordinary fellowship of work and play; the people next door; the members of a family; the sharing in a common goal of some kind – but the point is the same. *We only grow through relationships*. We pine without contact – like Gerry, or like that Prodigal Son, or like Adam without Eve.

All this is obvious from ordinary human experience. And the Bible can be approached from that point of view: as a book that illuminates what we already experience. If we come to the Bible remembering the longing for relationship which is so simple and so central, we find in fact that its pages are full of that same theme of relationship. One could easily sum up the Bible vision as saying that *God reaches out in relationship to humanity*. But all the images the Bible uses to capture that reaching out are taken from human experience – they are of fidelity or broken fidelity, of friendship, parenthood, and so on.

This first chapter has had one simple point to make – that being on one's own is never the whole story. In all the important things of life, even in solitude itself, we are shaped by relationships and we are made to grow through relationships. That hunger is there and it is a sign of something put into our hearts by God. Not only can I not be a Christian on my own, I cannot be a person on my own. The wrong kind of solitude (again that of Gerry or the Prodigal) leaves a person cramped, handicapped, unalive. In all the important things of life we need one another. And being a Christian *is* one of the important things of life.

FOR REFLECTION

You can let your own memories be the springboard for prayer, especially your memories of painful loneliness of one kind or another.

Can you identify some 'pigsty' moments? Times when you came up against emptiness or guilt or something close to despair? Times when you realised that you needed to 'go home', that you needed the courage to turn towards somebody?

Re-enter those memories slowly, quietly, without rush. Visit the feelings gently. Get in touch with something of your own story. Inside those experiences is the beginning of an answer to our question, 'Can I be a Christian on my own?'.

PRAYER

Lord, I look on this mess, this pigsty. How have I landed here? Is it because I cut myself off from others? I wanted to go off on my own. I thought that was the way to happiness. But now I know better.

I've never been so hungry. I know what I lack. I know what I need. I need something of home. I need others and I need you.

But the surprise of this story is that you know all this. You are waiting for me to turn again. You are running down the road to welcome me back from this false loneliness. You are the Lord of life and life is in the embrace of welcome, in the silence that understands and heals. There is no need for words. Just to be there with you, no longer alone.

Invitation to Community

ON THE SCHOOL RETREAT, John, a small fellow of seventeen, refused to take part in any of the exercises to begin with. He sat by himself, looking out the window. He looked angry, afraid – and lonely. Everyone was conscious of him as we went through the first session of the retreat, and we tried to get him to join in one or two of the conversations. But he was shy and unwilling, and you would have thought he would like to be anywhere but in the group. Another time you'd see him wanting to join in. During supper he livened up at times, mixed with the group on the retreat, boys and girls of his own age, who were from ten different schools. Then, as the evening went on, we could see him joining in everything and really getting into the retreat.

He explained why afterwards. 'When I came into the room', he said, 'and saw all the posh ones from . . . (mentioning a well-known wealthy school), I just clammed up. They made me feel small, with their accents and their expensive clothes. I felt like a fool, and just went into myself. Couldn't bring myself to talk to them. And I felt lousy. Went down to the tea even worse than when I came in. But then a few of them started talking to me and we got into a talk on school and leaving school, and they were listening to me. I realised that what I had to say was as good as anyone. I started feeling I had something they hadn't got and I was as good as any of them. And my faith means more to me going off now from the retreat. It was real community, being a group together. That's God for me. First time I got anything out of the Mass. Never thought I'd be saying that.'

John found a space on this retreat where others listened to him; thus he felt valued in himself. He found a space also where he could speak, and puzzle out some problems of his life and faith in an atmosphere where he wasn't being judged. He also found a space for prayer which touched his own desire for prayer, even though he mightn't have named it like that, and brought God alive in his own language and his own experience. The Eucharist was probably something like the incident in John 21 which will be examined later. Much of what John experienced on these few days are the marks of a Christian group. Can we find from this example and from the gospel what are the pillars and the qualities of a Christian community?

Later on, Jesus revealed himself again to the disciples. It was by the Sea of Tiberias, and it happened like this: Simon Peter, Thomas called the Twin, Nathanael from Cana in Galilee, the sons of Zebedee and two more of his disciples were together. Simon Peter said, 'I'm going fishing.' They replied, 'We'll come with you.' They went out and got into the boat but caught nothing that night.

When it was already light, there stood Jesus on the shore, though the disciples did not realise that it was Jesus. Jesus called out, 'Haven't you caught anything, friends?' And when they answered, 'No,' he said, 'Throw the net out to starboard and you'll find something.' So they threw the net out and could not haul it in because of the quantity of fish. The disciple whom Jesus loved said to Peter, 'It is the Lord.' At these words, 'It is the Lord,' Simon Peter tied his outer garment round him (for he had nothing on) and jumped into the water. The other disciples came on in the boat, towing the net with the fish; they were only about a hundred yards from land.

As soon as they came ashore they saw that there was some bread there and a charcoal fire with fish cooking on it. Jesus said, 'Bring some of the fish you have just caught.' Simon Peter went aboard and dragged the net ashore, full of big fish, one hundred and fifty-three of them; and in spite of there being so many the net was not broken. Jesus said to them, 'Come and have breakfast.' None of the disciples was bold enough to ask, 'Who are you?'. They knew quite well it was the Lord. Jesus then stepped forward, took the bread and gave it to them, and the same with the fish. This was the third time that Jesus revealed himself to the disciples after rising from the dead.

(John 21:1–14)

This incident where Jesus meets some of the apostles on the beach after the resurrection gives a picture of community. For prayer, this 'fantasy' exercise where you try to put yourself into the story may be helpful:

Become quiet and relax within yourself . . . maybe listen to the sounds you can hear for one or two minutes . . . just becoming quiet . . . then picture a beach you like . . . imagine yourself walking on this beach in the early morning just as the sun is rising . . . feel the air on your face, on your hands, on your feet as you walk through the sand . . . look around . . . how do you feel as you watch the sun rising? . . . you look up the beach and you see a group of people around a small fire . . . you wonder who's there . . . you walk towards it and you see people you know . . . a few friends . . . family . . . people who are friends in faith . . . Jesus is there in the middle of them . . . you wonder will you join them . . . pause for a moment . . . watch Jesus . . . what's he like? . . . the risen Lord . . . gives them some bread . . . and some fish from the fire . . . see him giving this to them . . . one by one . . . people you like and love . . . people you have something against . . . who like you . . . who don't like you . . . then Jesus looks at you and invites you to the group . . . move towards him . . . take the bread from him . . . and a piece of fish . . . let him smile at you . . . forgiving you . . . welcoming you . . . how do you feel? . . . what would you like to say to each of the people there? . . . what would you like to say to Jesus? . . . stay there now at the fire with them and with Jesus . . . notice that this is community . . . reconciliation among the group like among the apostles at the first breakfast on the beach . . . centred around Jesus and in the Eucharist . . . share now what's in your heart with the Lord and let him share what's in his heart for you.

The qualities of community in this incident are our relationship with Jesus (prayer), Eucharist, friendship, reconciliation with Jesus and with one another. The promise of service to people is highlighted later in the book, when we see how, in a Christian community, people care for God, for themselves, for each other and for the wider community.

Another essential pillar of the community is the commitment of each person to the group. The choice Peter made was made in the presence of the others when Jesus asked him to 'feed my lambs . . . feed my sheep' (John 21:15–19). Christian community is a group to which each is committed; it is more than a group to which each belongs. It cannot be a 'hit and miss', or 'hit and run', commitment, but each member must know that the others have decided to give this initiative all they have for whatever length of time they are together, be it two days or two years or a lifetime.

People all over the world will tell you of the difference it made to their lives when they found a vibrant group of Christians who made honest and sincere efforts to share their faith together. This is the experience of young volunteers in groups which live and work among the poor for a year or two, of religious communities who make a real effort at honestly shared life, and of prayer, reflection and social action groups who meet on a regular basis in parishes, retreat centres or schools.

What these people say goes like this: 'I couldn't go near Confession until I went to one of the community Penance Services for Christmas, and when I saw everyone going to Confession, and you could see them talking to a priest, then I felt God was real, and I went to Confession.' Or, 'I found a real life in my faith when I went to a prayer meeting.' Or, 'The retreat helped me to realise I wasn't on my own when I had problems with God or at home.'

Married people find this support in groups like Marriage Encounter and Teams of Our Lady which give them space and refreshment for their own married and family commitment. Priests find the same in groups like the Jesus Caritas fraternities which meet monthly for prayer, personal sharing and a meal. In such groups you generally find these 'pillars' of community, and when things may not be going well in them, a look to see if these pillars are all there, or if one is there more than another, can be helpful. For example a group that is over-concerned with personal growth will find itself becoming unbalanced and a bit narcissistic while a group over-concerned with social action without prayer or personal growth may get burned out.

We all draw enthusiasm and life within a Christian group both from the group itself and from Christ. Each of us has our own personal relationship with Jesus. A comparison of the life of the apostles at the Passion of Jesus and after the resurrection highlights some of the reality of isolation and of community in their lives, and can highlight the same thing for us.

You might see in this appearance of Jesus after the resurrection ways given to the apostles of *sustaining their vocation*. It suggests that prayer, community, Eucharist, reconciliation and service are among the principal means of sustaining the Christian vision.

For Christian life does not grow just by itself. In our age, often called the 'me-generation', particularly in the so-called first world, Narcissus, the mythical figure who had fallen in love with the image of himself he saw reflected in a lake, could be a 'patron saint'. The Church itself is called to challenge a privatised spirituality: the call to forgiveness and to reconciliation, to equality and justice, hold equal importance with the call to weekly Eucharist and private prayer.

This may bring into question the quality of our time together. Does Christian Sunday liturgy depress rather than activate our enthusiasm for Christ? Sometimes our Christian prayer gatherings promote a private 'me and God' spirituality. But it need not be like that. As ministers of the gospel we try to create among ourselves occasions like the 'beach breakfast': an experience of reconciliation and of forgiveness, of joy and of peace, of thanksgiving and of being really called into the service of God, a moment when you know 'you cannot be a Christian on your own'.

The picture of the early Church in John 21 shows the means it discovered for sustaining the desire for a real and loving following of Christ. It is together around the Eucharist, in fellowship and in friendship, with Jesus and with each other, that we find the sustenance for our Christian growth.

FOR REFLECTION

1. Recall a time in your own life when community helped . . . when a group of Christians helped you at a bad time, for example in bereavement or anxiety.
2. Have you found the authentic celebration of the Sacraments – especially of Reconciliation and the Eucharist – a point of growth in your own faith?

3. Recall the people who have been significant in your 'community of believers'. Your parents and your children, grandparents and grandchildren, other family and friends, teachers, parishioners, priests and religious: imagine these people as being around the fire with you on the beach with Jesus!
4. If you are a member of any group, reflect which pillars and qualities of a Christian community are strong in the group.

PRAYER

Give me, Lord, a heart for others;
enliven my feelings and thoughts with compassion
and with sympathy for others.
Let me really believe, in my heart and mind,
that faith and hope and Christian love grow in community.

Help our family and community, our parish and neighbourhood
to live and work in the spirit of the gospel.

And make me, Lord, an instrument of community
and a sign of God
in the way I look on others and relate to them,
speak to others and listen to them
work with others, and for them.

In this way may I be a person for others,
a person for God.

Amen.

Family and Faith

JEAN, A VIVACIOUS SEVENTEEN-YEAR-OLD, was in a group of young people on a 'Discovery' evening. They were talking about faith and family, and Jean talked about her relationship with her parents. It seemed a healthy relationship in which they could all talk personally and openly.

Jean had the usual questions every young person has about sexuality and about relationships with boys, but during the group session on this subject, she told us that she had learned a lot from her parents talking to her honestly about their own relationships when they were her age. They had obviously talked about their own conflicts and questions about sexual expression and the meaning of sexuality, and also about their marriage. This was better she thought than many of the formal classes she had on sexuality and marriage in school.

Peter, an eighteen-year-old who was somewhat shy in talking about personal questions, was in a group of young people talking about faith, and how they were finding different aspects of their faith. Gradually the talk got around to prayer, which is not something often talked about. Peter told us that he prayed every night before going to bed: a habit he had got from his father who had died when he was eleven, but who had prayed with him every night before he went to sleep.

He went down with them then and came to Nazareth and lived under their authority. His mother stored up all these things in her heart. And Jesus increased in wisdom, in stature, and in favour with God and with people.

(Luke 2:51–2)

Near the cross of Jesus stood his mother and his mother's sister, Mary the wife of Clopas, and Mary of Magdala. Seeing his mother and the disciple whom he loved standing near her, Jesus said to his mother, 'Woman, this is your son.' Then to the disciple he said, 'This is your mother.' And from that hour the disciple took her into his home.

(John 19:25–7)

It was at this time that Jesus came from Nazareth in Galilee and was baptised in the Jordan by John.

(Mark 1:9)

Another incident described in three of the four gospels shows that Jesus' ties with home were broken so that he could fulfil the mission given him by God:

He was still speaking to the crowds when suddenly his mother and his brothers were standing outside and were anxious to have a word with him. But to the man who told him this, Jesus replied, 'Who is my mother? Who are my brothers?' And stretching out his hand towards his disciples he said, 'Here are my mother and my brothers. Anyone who does the will of my Father in heaven is my brother and sister and mother.'

(Matthew 12:46–8)

Is it strange that the gospel passes on so little of Jesus' family life? A few phrases here and there give an impression of it, but much is missing. There is nothing at all about his relationship with Joseph, for example. The family life of Jesus shows that he grew in the ordinary way of humans: he was born and he lived with his parents for the first thirty years of his life. We know also that he had to find his independence from his home and his kin. And that he maintained a very close relationship with his mother, who was present at his death, and was a key figure in the first years of the Church: we notice she was in the upper room for the first Pentecost. He must have gone through many family experiences such as getting a job, the death of Joseph, and leaving home.

The following imaginative meditation may fill out what is said so sparsely by the evangelists: Jesus' leaving home and his journey to baptism in the Jordan. His baptism is a sign that he fully enters into the community of believers of his own time.

Imagine Jesus leaving home . . . he is about thirty . . . a healthy young man leaving Nazareth and going towards the river Jordan where John is baptising . . . watch him leaving Mary . . . saying goodbye at the door of their house . . . a hug and a kiss to his mother . . . he must now go full time 'about his Father's business' . . . he walks alone along the road . . . a sunny day and you can see the river Jordan in the distance . . . but he stops for a while and sits down to think . . . you are watching him . . . what do you think he might be grateful to his mother for . . . the years of care . . . the way she cooked for him . . . cleaned for him . . . loved him . . . supported him when Joseph died . . . what do you think he might be grateful for? . . . the prayers she taught him . . . learning the Psalms from her . . . taught him about the prophets and the Scriptures . . . gave him ways of believing in his Father . . . taught him some of the Scripture which he will now teach 'with authority' to others . . . talk to him yourself about what you're grateful to your own family for . . . let your talk flow . . . or write it in a letter to him . . . all you are thankful to your family for . . . and think also of your faith and what they gave you of faith . . . even talk to him about what is different in your faith, for you must leave your family as he did . . . spend some time with this . . . no hurry . . . end when you wish with the *Our Father*.

The family is the first 'community of faith'. It has been called the 'domestic church'. In it we first learn of love, the closest reality we find to the mystery of God. We learn about love from how we see it in our parents and family, and how we experience it for ourselves. Our emotional memories of love influence forever how we think of God, for God is love.

A child whose father is kind can relate to a kind father-God; the child whose only image of father is a drunken, violent man has trouble relating to a father-image of God. Peter learned to pray in his family: he learned a habit of prayer, a way of praying and more important a gut-feeling about the importance of prayer. This was because his father prayed regularly.

Like Jean, our children learn about marriage from what they see of it in their home. If you asked a child, 'What is marriage?', she would reply most probably with some description of her parents' marriage. It is the same with other aspects of the Christian life. A child will learn more of the Church's approach to the poor from the way adult Christians, especially parents, treat the poor person at the door. As in Jean's conversation with her parents, children and adolescents learn attitudes to relationships and sexual behaviour, as well as feelings about their own sexuality, from the words, tones and moods they pick up from their parents.

Faith is caught in the family, not just taught. Other influences will sometimes over-ride the influence of the family later on, but the deepest roots of faith begin there. Even if behaviour and practice is divergent among the generations, the deeper values we live by begin in the family.

Family life suffers many strains today. Greater mobility means that family members live further away from each other. Mothers and fathers may not see their adult children, or their grandchildren: you could live in the same city and still be more than two hours' drive from home.

In some ways, modern culture doesn't support family life. Sexuality can be lightly valued. Peer pressure among teenagers is strong, and parents can find themselves losing contact with their children at an age when they need guidance. The media often deals lightly with the values of family life, and portrays a world of easy divorce and casual relationships.

With such pressures, it is important to hold on to our belief that children learn about many important areas of life very early in their lives: patterns of love, anger, trust, faith, hope, fear, anxiety and the gamut of human emotions and responses so central to commitment and to religion, as well as to friendship, marriage and other deep commitments, are learned in the first years of life. The family is the first place one learns that 'I can't be a Christian on my own'.

The influence of the family on faith is both positive and negative. A young man said to me, 'I could believe in God if religion didn't make my mother so miserable.' Some practices have been ruined for children by the kind of emphasis placed on them when they were young. For example, some people want to ignore Lent, because of repressive memories of 'no sweets, no TV and no dessert until Lent is over'. It can be the same with family prayer, daily Mass or certain aspects of behaviour.

People discover their own responses to God and their own ways of faith, some of which are like those of their parents' and some of which are different. Adults can go through many struggles as they watch younger people make this journey of faith for themselves, but with the right approach, we can negotiate this journey more easily.

It is important for us to remember that everyone must find his or her own adult faith. Expressions of faith change in different cultures and ages. Most of us in our youth search for our own faith. We reject some of the faith of our fathers and mothers; we keep on some of what they have given us, and the roots are deep. But young people search to find their own authentic ways of praying, living, and believing.

Faith grows slowly and its development varies from person to person. Thus a difficult challenge for parents is to accept that each person – including their children – finds his or her own path to God; each path has its own contours, turnings and even sidetracks.

Parents find it difficult to see different ways of prayer, life and belief in their children without blaming themselves. This happens when they hear their children have stopped going to church, are living with a boyfriend or girlfriend, or have difficulties believing in some areas of faith.

It can lead into anger (where have they gone wrong?), guilt (where have we gone wrong?), or confusion (where have we all gone wrong?). No parent is perfect, and in every family mistakes have been made in bringing up children. Every priest and teacher feels the same at times.

But parents are not the only agents of faith for their children. Members of the same family show different depths of faith and of practice. One may be a priest, while another is non-practising: in the one family, there may be many faiths. Faith is influenced by peers, by school, church, the culture in which we live and our experiences of life.

Young people, for their part, need to be able to ask honestly what in their parents' faith is good and worth keeping. Practice can be abandoned for many reasons, and mature growth in faith means we should try to be honest in admitting to laziness, to resentment against authority and to peer pressure, as well as searching for personal maturity and sincere faith.

FOR REFLECTION

1. Recall the gifts of life you have had from your family: recall the people in your family . . . think of them . . . one by one . . . let different memories come to mind . . . try first to recall those for which you are grateful . . . feel the gratitude for your mother . . . father . . . brothers . . . sisters . . . thank God in your own words or silently for them.

   Recall memories that are painful . . . pray for the people . . . see them in the presence of God and pray for them . . . hand them over and try to ask for healing of your own hurt.
2. How is your own faith different from your parents' faith? What is different in how you practice your faith, in your beliefs, in the way you pray, and in your religious sense? Are you happy with the changes? Have you lost anything of your parents' faith which you think is valuable?

PRAYER

Lord, you are the Source of all life and love
and you have loved me and given me life through my family.
May I be truly grateful for all they have done for me;
bless them: father, mother, brothers, sisters (name them).
May I forgive and understand hurts and harm in our family
for in the closeness of family life we hurt each other.
Help me forgive any wrongs, and may they forgive me.

Bless family life and enrich families with your love;
may we your people promote the good of the family
and may your Church supply what is missing
to some who are victims of unhappy and broken marriages,
or whose parents cannot take care of them.

May love be valued and promoted among us
and may we know that when we find love
we find you, Lord God, the source of all love.

Leave Me Alone

MARK AND JOE were friends of long standing – from having been in primary school together. Now they were both nineteen, sharing a flat while they mixed part-time jobs with part-time studies. But for several months now Mark had become withdrawn and cynical. Joe felt that the old bridges between them were fast disappearing, and that he could not reach him any more. Mark's frequent drinking was part of it, and sometimes the use of drugs, but Joe was sure that these were only symptoms of some deeper unhappiness that he did not know about. It was not like Mark to be so closed or hard. As regards girlfriends, Mark had previously had a few longish relationships, but now he seemed to be having one girlfriend after another in rapid succession, and without any apparent sense of enjoyment.

What could Joe do? He knew what he would like to do, but the moment never seemed right. Mark needed someone who would open the doors of hope for him again, and Joe was sure that he knew the right person. But he had never even mentioned Sister Christine to Mark. Joe had met her through his mother a few months ago and this old nun had had an immediate effect on him. There was nothing dramatic about her and yet Joe at once felt himself in the presence of someone special. She lived in a community for handicapped people and had a real 'way' with them. Quite simply, she loved them and they her. And she seemed to have plenty of attention and wisdom left over for everybody else as well. If only he could get Mark to meet Sister Christine! But Joe was afraid of the usual brush-off, of being told, *leave me alone . . .*

This is a real life story, which in fact ended happily: Christine did eventually 'reach' Mark, but the details of how it happened do not matter here. The cynicism of Mark, the concern of Joe and the healing qualities of Christine all find their parallels in the following marvellous drama in the gospel. As you read it, notice how one friend brings another to Jesus. In fact it is the first fairly detailed account that we have in John's gospel of Jesus interacting with somebody and of the change he brought about in that other person.

The next day, after Jesus had decided to leave for Galilee, he met Philip and said, 'Follow me'. Philip came from the same town, Bethsaida, as Andrew and Peter. Philip found Nathanael and said to him, 'We have found the one Moses wrote about in the Law, the one about whom the prophets wrote: he is Jesus son of Joseph, from Nazareth'. 'From Nazareth?' said Nathanael. 'Can anything good come from that place?' 'Come and see' replied Philip. When Jesus saw Nathanael coming he said of him, 'There is an Israelite who deserves the name, incapable of deceit'. 'How do you know me?' said Nathanael. 'Before Philip came to call you,' said Jesus 'I saw you under the fig tree.' Nathanael answered, 'Rabbi, you are the Son of God, you are the King of Israel'. Jesus replied, 'You believe that just because I said: I saw you under the fig tree. You will see greater things than that.'

(John 1:43–50)

Let us read this episode in the light of our earlier story.

It helps to put flesh on the skeleton tale that we have in the gospel, and yet every little step as recounted by John is significant. It seems that where you come from can have an impact on your openness to faith. We are told that Philip came from the same town as two of the apostles. And so when Jesus met Philip his invitation to follow him seems to have been received immediately, without hesitation. Perhaps Philip knew of Jesus already, and was even hoping to be able to join his group of friends.

No sooner does he join up with Jesus than Philip thinks of Nathanael. Seemingly Nathanael was not from Bethsaida; at any rate he seems to have been a much tougher nut to crack than his friend Philip, who was immediately responsive to Jesus. We are to learn later that Nathanael was a serious searcher, but on the surface he was a bit of a sceptic. Something had made him wary – just as something had made Mark in our story hard and sour. Philip even appears a little innocent in his approach to him. He arrives, seemingly all enthusiastic about Jesus, to tell Nathanael the great news. And, an extraordinary thing for any Jew to say to another, he is telling him that the long wait is over, that the ancient hopes raised through Moses and the prophets have been fulfilled, that the Messiah has in fact come, and that he, Philip, has actually found him and become one of his disciples. It is a lot to claim.

So no wonder Nathanael's first response is a little dubious, even a bit cynical about Nazareth: 'Can anything good come from that place?' Remember the same mood in Mark. Don't we all tend to 'knock' things that seem too good to be true, especially when we are in a certain hurt or withdrawn mood? Nathanael's resistance through sarcasm is alive and well and serves as a shield for all of us at times. And people learn not to push us when we are prickly.

But Philip is not to be put off so easily. He comes right back with a challenge: you needn't believe me, come and see for yourself. Behind the simple words of the gospel lies a whole reservoir of rich meaning. Right through John's gospel the words 'come and see' recur like a refrain; they are simple words but they accumulate power and significance. *Come* does not mean just walking down the road. *See* does not mean just having a good look. It is an invitation to be truly present, to come with an attitude of reverence and hunger, and so to be open to a new kind of seeing. It is also an invitation to experience faith for yourself. If Nathanael had believed Philip, that would not necessarily be faith. It could be belief – on the authority of his friend. But faith is rooted in something more personal, an encounter with Jesus. And that is what the whole story is leading towards.

From now on every little detail of the gospel story seems marvellous – as indeed they have been up to now. The next move, so to speak, comes from Jesus. Notice that again those little words turn up again: when Jesus *saw* Nathanael *coming*, he spoke of him as a genuine Israelite, as somebody of utter honesty. Notice first of all the significance of those repeated words. It is in a deep sense that Jesus *sees* Nathanael *coming*. Jesus throughout this gospel is the one who can see what is really in people's hearts (John 2:25). Here he sees the hope and the hunger behind the tough facade that Nathanael had shown to Philip. He sees the *coming*, in the sense of the coming out into the open of this man of secret longing. He sees the goodness in him, perhaps in a way that no one else ever did. And what he says seems to surprise and even shock Nathanael, who says in words that sound so modern, 'How do you know me'?

Once again, in the rich poetry that is Scripture, this question is full of echoes. How are we known by God? It echoes that extraordinary Psalm 139 evoking the way in which God knows everyone, with total thoroughness and total love:

you know when I sit, when I rise,
you understand my thoughts from afar . . .
Such amazing knowledge is beyond me,
a height to which I cannot attain . . .
For so many marvels I thank you;
a wonder am I, and all your works are wonders . . .
You knew me through and through . . .

Returning to the gospel story, Nathanael received a surprisingly warm welcome from Jesus, words of appreciation, of recognition of his goodness; and perhaps this is something that he is shy to admit even to himself. Hence his question. 'Can I trust this man and his welcome?', he seems to be asking. Don't we all feel a certain surprise and even doubt when the stale old words 'God loves you' manage to escape from cliché and become truly personal? But there is more to come in this short but strangely detailed story. The reply of Jesus to Nathanael is like a secret message, because it refers to something that perhaps only Nathanael himself could understand. In this way it serves as a proof of how well Jesus knows him. It is the moment in the story which goes beyond Philip. 'Before Philip called you, I saw you under the fig tree.' It is as if Jesus is saying to Nathanael: you may think that I heard about you from your good friend Philip. No, in fact, I have known you in a different way altogether. Philip's friendship has been crucial in bringing us together, but you are now in the presence of somebody who knows you more than any friend.

And what are we to make of this mention of the fig tree? The Scripture scholars make suggestions but nobody is certain – and indeed that may be just as well because it leaves the moment open to being a symbol of how we are known by God in our depths. It seems that to sit under the fig tree was sometimes thought of as the place of meditation, and in this sense to do so would be for Nathanael a gesture of prayer, even of hoping for the Messiah. It is as if he had a secret life of longing for a

Saviour but that he was shy of talking about it – even to his friend Philip. Don't many people in fact have a shy spiritual side to them, sometimes not even known to their best friends? And yet Philip is the kind of good friend who could guess at what he had never been told, and so he could ignore Nathanael's initial tendency to sneer at Nazareth. But it is Jesus, as a different kind of friend, who goes beyond guessing into knowing, and into proving that he knows – about the fig tree and whatever hidden hunger or lonely struggle it conjures up for Nathanael.

Even if we cannot be sure about the exact significance of the fig tree, there is no doubt about what the mention of it provokes from Nathanael – nothing less than an amazing cry of faith: 'You are the Son of God.' He has come a long way from the distrust and pessimism of his first response to Philip. And in fact the reply of Jesus at this stage points to so much more awaiting him. It is as if Jesus is smiling at the huge jump that Nathanael has made because of something small and promising him an even greater road ahead. Now that Nathanael has arrived at the personal recognition that is faith, a whole adventure opens up, one that goes beyond this life itself into a vision of God. 'You believe that just because I said I saw you under the fig tree. You are going to see greater things than that . . . you will see heaven open.'

What began with the invitation of a friend has become something extraordinary, a vision that reaches out to eternity and to God. Two truths interact here. One is the essential need for friendship, for a Philip who can help towards the possibility of faith. The other is that the encounter with Jesus can be deeeply personal, beyond the realm of human friendship or community. To return to the title of this book, perhaps we have to give a fuller answer in the light of this story. I cannot be a Christian on my own because I always need others to lead me towards Jesus, to point him out to me, to awaken my hopes. Yet at the heart of the adventure of faith is a certain core of being 'on one's own', but with Jesus. And as we can see in other sections of this book, Jesus never invites us to come and cling to him alone: he always sends us back to others, back into the needy world with a mission of love.

FOR REFLECTION

1. Think of times when you made yourself hard for others to reach. Think of certain friends who have the knack of sidestepping those shields of your sulks. Because of them you emerged from dark and lonely moods. Their company did the trick, and drew you out of your hurt, small self. Perhaps at times those others did not even realise they were helping to raise your spirits.
2. Or put yourself on the other side of the story. Think of occasions when you were like Joe – knowing that some friend was a bit lost and wanting to find the key that would open up some new horizon. Perhaps you would love to help somebody discover faith in Christ. Like Philip again.

As in all the invitations at the end of these chapters, don't rush. Don't do it with the top of your head. Give it time. Otherwise it will never catch fire: it will never draw you to a threshold of prayer or wonder. The Scriptures need to be read like love-letters, slowly and often, savouring the words of the Beloved.

In this way you can take that Nathanael story and pause on each sentence. Some will speak deeply to you, if you let them. They will remind you of desires within you. Or else you could take Psalm 139, which was mentioned earlier, and go through it gently as a realisation of how God understands you – something that is both a source of fearful amazement and yet surrendering gratitude for the poet of that psalm.

PRAYER

Imagine how Nathanael might pray, later on that day, of his faith encounter with Jesus. Something like this perhaps:

Lord Jesus, looking back on today, I'm overwhelmed by the wonder of it. So often I sat under my lonely fig tree, doing my official prayer for a Messiah 'some day'. I didn't really imagine that 'some day' would become 'today', that the future I dreamed would become the present and the person I met in you. Lord, I also give thanks for Philip. Without him I would never have found you. Without his patience I would have stayed in my grumpiness. Thanks to you, and thanks for the Philip people in my life too.

Ministry with Others

BILLY WAS ON THE STAFF of the retreat house I worked in for a number of years. A shy priest, he had a very warm welcome for everyone who came to the centre. You would not by any manner of means call him a good preacher, nor a leader of a retreat group. He had however what some of the busier people of the house lacked: a sensitivity for letting everyone who came to the house know that they were welcome.

The depth and sincerity of his welcome brought into our house an atmosphere of healing, acceptance, personal relationship. People noticed that, and were grateful that he was always there, ready with a cup of coffee or tea, a smile, a joke, and grateful too that he never made demands on them. Billy died at thirty-five, a young priest who had given more to people than he ever knew. The big crowd at his funeral was a tribute to the great gift he was to us, and sadly it took his death for us to properly realise his contribution to our youth centre.

Looking up, Jesus saw the crowds approaching and said to Philip, 'Where can we buy some bread for these people to eat?' He said this only to put Philip to the test; he himself knew exactly what he was going to do. Philip answered, 'Two hundred denarii would not buy enough to give them a little piece each.' One of his disciples, Andrew, Simon Peter's brother, said, 'Here is a small boy with five barley loaves and two fish; but what is that among so many?' Jesus said to them, 'Make the people sit down.' There was plenty of grass there and as many as five thousand men sat down. Then Jesus took the loaves, gave thanks, and distributed them to those who were sitting there; he did the same with the fish, distributing as much as they wanted. When they had eaten enough he said to the disciples, 'Pick up the pieces left over, so that nothing is wasted.' So they picked them up and filled twelve large baskets with scraps left over from the meal of five barley loaves.

(John 6:5–13)

The apostles were asked to feed the crowds; all they could find were the five loaves and two fish which had been brought for his lunch by a boy in the crowd. Can you imagine Jesus going to this lad and asking him for his help in feeding the crowd. 'With my little lunch-box?', he might say. 'With only what I have?' Yet the work of Jesus was done with all the help this boy could give, even though it looked little from the outside.

That's often the way with us. We think that what we have to bring to Jesus would be so little. Many people when they are asked, for example, to visit the sick or the shut-in people of a parish, say 'But what can I do? I can only listen to a kid's troubles or bring a meal or type the newsletter or drive someone to Mass.'

No matter what sort of service we offer, it is always appreciated if it is personal: giving something in a way that respects another's dignity. Many people can offer welfare, advice, money, even counselling on a professional level. Many professionals are men and women of great compassion; some are not, and the poor of the world, the dispossessed and the needy will always need compassionate people who can care with the care of Jesus. Most of us with some prayer, good listening, tolerance and patience can do it, and so grow in our unselfishness. All of us, by being the people we are, can be of service in God's kingdom.

For those who can listen – let them listen. For those who can drive and bring meals on wheels – let them do so. For those who can change the laws of a country in politics – let them do so. All of us can play our part in the kingdom of God. Our natural ability as well as some training and reflection on our abilities can make us instruments of peace, compassion, justice and love in the world.

At times we find it hard to believe in ourselves. We wonder if we have much to offer. A person finds he or she cannot volunteer for some item of service and work for others because of a lack of self-confidence, an inferiority complex, or a poor self-image – call it what you like. It is the aspect of our personality which makes us say – before we even examine the situation – '*I* couldn't do that'. In various ways we can help each other grow in self-esteem.

Now it happened that he was standing one day by the Lake of Gennesaret, with the crowd pressing round him listening to the word of God, when he caught sight of two boats at the water's edge. The fishermen had got out of them and were washing their nets. He got into one of the boats – it was Simon's – and asked him to put out a little from the shore. Then he sat down and taught the crowds from the boat.

When he had finished speaking he said to Simon, 'Put out into deep water and pay out your nets for a catch.' Simon replied, 'Master, we worked hard all night long and caught nothing, but if you say so, I will pay out the nets.' And when they had done this, they netted such a huge number of fish that their nets began to tear, so they signalled to their companions in the other boat to come and help them; when these came, they filled both boats to sinking point.

When Simon Peter saw this he fell at the knees of Jesus saying, 'Leave me, Lord, I am a sinful man.' For he and all his companions were completely awestruck at the catch they had made; so also were James and John, sons of Zebedee, who were Simon's partners. But Jesus said to Simon, 'Do not be afraid; from now on it is people you will be catching.' Then bringing their boats back to land they left everything and followed him.

(Luke 5:1–11)

A key insight in this story is that the apostles needed 'other boats' to bring in the fish. It is true that while each of us has our own gifts to use in the service of God, we generally serve him alongside other people. Everyone who has tried to work in the service of God and of the gospel of Jesus Christ has gathered others around him or her to do so. From the smallest Vincent de Paul conference in the smallest parish, to a big religious movement like l'Arche, all involve us in working with others, using the contributions of each person's gifts and talents. Just as you cannot live as a Christian on your own, neither can you work as a Christian on your own.

Such groups need to help each other become good helpers. Just as religious orders have times of training and formation – the aim of which is to enable members to use their talents to the best in the service of God – so also every group needs to spend some time developing the talents of each member.

For example, people working among the very poor can share insights and methods of helping disadvantaged people. If you are working to help the bereaved, you need some training in bereavement counselling, while among teenagers you will need some training and knowledge of adolescent development. Your expertise and talent in your service are increased by working alongside others in the same field.

The work of three people together is more effective than the work of the same three people on their own. The community that exists between them, the shared vision and interest, is almost like another person; we find a mysterious element in working together that adds to the work we do.

This means trying to transcend the difficulties of co-operation – jealousies, fears, anxieties, competitiveness – that come into our work together. These are examined later in the book in the chapter on blocks to community.

Important blocks to working together are intolerance and lack of self-confidence. One prevents us seeing the good things another can do, the other prevents us seeing our own good points. Intolerance of others can come through fear of others' talents or jealousy of what they can do (you may notice this in the small circle of a folk-group or choir!). Or it may manifest itself in a strong inability to deal with others' differences of opinion.

We need to help each other keep our motivation. I might organise a scheme to help the unemployed, for example, and then find I like the admiration of the public more than the people I set out to help. Let's always have ways in our service-groups of refreshing the vision of the gospel which led us into the service of the Lord in the first place, ways that can help us recommit ourselves to what we want to do in his service.

The story of Peter and the others in Luke 5:1–11 shows the willingness of the Lord to work with the person who is open to him, and shows the call of the Lord to work together, seen in the way Peter has to go to the other boats if the work is to be completed. You don't work for God on your own. We fish together, we think together to decide how and where to work best for God. We need each other's help both to fish and to continue with the fishing we began.

FOR REFLECTION

1. Recall times that you were helped in your service of God by the people you worked with; they may have helped you in a time of discouragement or when you wanted to give up. Think of them – and the situations – one by one – don't hurry to get through a lot. Feel your need of helpers.
2. Another aspect of these stories is that together we trust in the Lord. Can you recall times of trusting that God would help you in your work for him? Or got through times when you felt it was all a waste but in the end you saw that some good had come out of all your efforts? Recall these times – slowly – feel your trust in God's companionship with you in what you are trying to do for him.

PRAYER

Lord, help us work together in your service.
Help us develop and encourage the talents of everyone
and to overcome jealousy and envy with your love.
We know that two or more hearts united in friendship
can work more effectively for you
than when we work alone.
Give us the encouragement of each other's
wishes and hopes and promises to serve you.
May we with our companions
be people desiring to work for you
and for those of your people in need.

Blocks to Community

A MAN AND A WOMAN MET one day in the village. Both were good people and did their best to do good in their own way. The woman lived up the mountain and spent a lot of time visiting people who were housebound or sick, bringing food or just spending time with them. The man lived in the village and was a teacher, keen on his work and concerned for the children. They knew each other a little but never met. One day, the story goes, they met and the woman said she often looked down from the mountain and thought how much good the teacher did and that she would like to be able to be a teacher and she often thought at night about how much more she could do for God if she were a teacher. The man said, 'Funny, I often look up at the mountain and think that you do so much good, visiting the sick and just spending time with them, and I think how much better I could be if I spent time with the sick like you do.' And they both realised that human beings are strange creatures in how they think, how they compare themselves to each other and don't see the good they're doing themselves because they only see the good someone else is doing.

One of the blocks to growth within a Christian group is when we compare ourselves to others in the group. Follow our story further and you would find jealousy growing, or if they tried to work together, snide comments and difficult group meetings, rooted in self-doubt and competitiveness. In a true Christian group each of us accepts our own personal strengths and limitations.

'Don't talk to me about the parable of the talents', a lady said after Mass on a day when the gospel of Matthew 25 had been read. 'I have no talents – can't sing in a choir, can't be a teacher, can't drive for meals on wheels. All I can do is love.' But isn't this the best talent of all, the gift least noticed but most valued in a group – that a person is a good listener, is compassionate and open-hearted?

When the other ten heard this they began to feel indignant with James and John. But Jesus called them to him and said to them, 'You know that among the gentiles those they call their rulers lord it over them, and their great men make their authority felt. Among you this is not to happen. No; anyone who wants to become great among you must be your servant, and anyone who wants to be first among you must be slave to all. For the Son of man himself came not to be served but to serve, and to give his life as a ransom for many.'

(Mark 10:41–5)

Competitiveness in a group is bound to happen: people compete with each other for success, for approval, for being first (and being last!), for all sorts of rewards. The apostles competed for being Jesus' favourite, for being the most powerful healer, for knowing the most. Jesus turns many of our all-too-human desires upside down. Many a Christian group – from folk-group or choir to worldwide missionary society – has been ruined by the jealousies and antipathies of its members, sometimes over very small matters. There would have been no feeding of the crowds if Peter and Andrew had been jealous of the boy who had the few loaves and fishes (John 6).

We are competitive because we are afraid of how others may appear better than we are. We are competitive because we need approval, and we need to be seen to be better than others. We are competitive because we are jealous of qualities others have. Some people are more competitive than others, but it is part of everyone's make up.

The gospel asks us to transcend competitiveness with the example of Jesus, who came 'not to be served but to serve', who washed his apostles' feet, who forgave to the end, and who saw the good in everyone.

The opposite of competitiveness is not sameness. Every group has its different talents and qualities, all the different talents of its members. A group is not meant to be uniform and similar in everything. Sometimes we put too much of an emphasis on sameness – saying the same things, and being fearful of people's individuality.

Jesus himself seems to have had a huge respect for the person and for individual differences. The sameness he asks for is on the inside: the desire to love and to serve God in his people so that 'we are either for him or against him'. He calls different people to different services: the apostles are called to a worldwide service, while the man from the tombs (Mark 5) whom he cured was not allowed to go with him but told to 'spread the word among your own people'.

There is also the block of shyness and privateness. We are not just community people: we each have our own private world. This private world is necessary. Some people through fear of trusting others, memories of bad experiences early in life, anxiety about what people would find out about them, are over-protective of themselves. Like Gerry in our first chapter, they hold themselves back when they really need to reach out.

Another block to Christian community can occur when people don't get the confident and trusting touch of another to help them break through walls of shyness which have been built up by others in the past. The community of Jesus hopes for trust: a trust based on the intrinsic worth of each person, and on our common relationship with Jesus. Each person in a Christian community is irreplaceable, and brings a unique gift to a group because they are who they are.

Not all gifts are the same, and at times some are more necessary than others. The apostles were enriched by each other's gifts. Peter's impetuousness was enriched by Mary's contemplativeness, and vice versa. The huge affection of Mary Magdalen and the mystical love of John complemented the early followers of Jesus. There is a realisation that everyone is a gift of God, for others. If we bring out that giftedness of ourselves, then the gift we are is more evident. Within a trusting relationship in which people affirm each other we can honestly talk about 'the Christ in you meeting the Christ in me'.

Jockeying for power and for favouritism, even the favouritism of God, can be a temptation in a Christian group. Jesus turns human ambition upside down. We are to shine as servants and be first in love. Power is a great temptation for people. They fear that others will have power over them, so they go for the first place, or they are personalities who just like being in charge. This drive towards power can ruin any Christian group, as it has often ruined good ventures within the Church.

A block to community may also be found within the culture we live in. The parable of the sower recalls the thorns into which the word of God is sown: 'Other seed fell among thorns, and the thorns grew up and choked them . . . The seed sown in thorns is someone who hears the word, but the worry of the world and the lure of riches choke the word and so it produces nothing' (Matthew 13:7, 22).

The thorns can be the elements of a culture which does not support the Christian message, and which can hamper the growth of a Christian group. Thorns may also be found within the Church itself which is always in need of renewal and purification in its understanding and practice to remain faithful to Jesus Christ.

Our culture stresses the dignity of the individual and a concern for equality and justice. Christian values of non-violence and of honesty are enshrined in many laws and constitutions. Christian groups and individual Christians need to be aware of the positive and negative effects of the culture in relation to the Christian gospel, for the world as we live in it is the stage of the gospel. Into this world the seed of God's Word is sown.

Many aspects of modern culture run counter to the gospel. The obsession with wealth seen in the demands for greater wealth at the expense of the poor is one example. Another is the demand for immediate gratification and for casual sexual relationships. There is mistrust of the possibility of the permanent in marriage and other choices which runs against Christian virtues like perseverance and commitment. In a world where we are taught to look after number one, community values cannot be encouraged.

Another barrier to community can even be the reality of the Church itself. Many people do not experience their Christianity in parishes, schools or otherwise as community-based or community-oriented. From the point of view of blocks to community, the image of the Church, poor in many places, may be underestimated.

The Church may be seen as the Pope and Bishops, as a place for prayer or the sacraments, as a calm port in a stormy world or a rock of certainty. The Church we need today is one which is in close touch with 'the joy and griefs, the hopes and frustrations of the modern world'. The Church of today is challenged by the words of St John: 'whoever does not love the brother whom he can see, cannot love God whom he has not seen' (1 John 4:20). The Church of today is called to walk within the world, almost like a pilgrim, listening to the concerns of the world and offering it the word of life.

A realistic summary of the concerns of the world in relation to the Church would include:

– the urgent hunger of our people for prayer and for meaning in life
– the inequality of the availability of the world's resources for all peoples
– the plight of refugees
– the frustrations and hopes of women
– the economic oppression of millions of people
– social injustices, unemployment and violence in developed countries
– ecological and environmental concerns of pollution and the destruction of natural resources.

These concerns, among many others, must be seen and heard to be essential concerns of the Church. Other aspects of Church life such as the democratisation of structures of authority; the place of women in the Church; the method of appointment of Church leaders; ecumenism on inter-church and inter-faith levels; the pluralism of attitudes, thought and moral action among Christians, among others, are issues of concern within the Church, which if not addressed weaken the sense of belonging many people, priests, religious and laity, feel towards the local and the universal Church.

FOR REFLECTION

Every Christian group needs its different members. Ask yourself:

1. Recall – by yourself or with someone you trust – the talents you have to offer in the group you are in. Are there talents you don't have which you'd like to possess, and can you allow others to use these in the group without being jealous?

2. Am I open to being helped in my group, or do I always have to be the helper?
3. Within the culture in which you live, you may notice elements which do not support the Christian gospel. Within the Church, what blocks a group doing what it wants to do for people? How is the energy of the group sapped or helped by the culture?

PRAYER

Lord God, source of community and source of good desires,
enlighten us in your truth and love:
enlighten us to know the full beauty of your gospel,
its vision of compassion and equality and love;
enlighten us to know the goodness of our world
its power, and beauty, and its love.
Enlighten us also to the pull of evil and the power of darkness
so that we can see when we are blocked in our efforts
of community and of honesty and of love
by the values of culture and of selfishness.

Be with us, Lord Jesus,
the Way to God the Father,
the Truth that gives meaning to life
and the Love which encourages our goodness,
for you, Lord Jesus, are
the Way, the Truth and the Life of God.

Discovering Church

ANNA WAS A SOVIET WOMAN of her generation, born in the tough years of the early 1950s and brought up with all the propaganda of communism. She never took it too seriously except in one respect – its adoration of science as the truth that had replaced the mythology of religion. So Anna set her heart on becoming a scientist and as time went on, she found herself climbing further and further up the ladder of success and specialisation, so much so that by the age of thirty she had become a distinguished university lecturer in physics.

Religion did not exist for Anna – unless one could call her devotion to science a religion. And yet the more she probed the frontier questions in physics, the more she realised that the older certainties were evaporating. Truth was much more mysterious than it had seemed to earlier physicists. She found herself drawn into philosophical questions that she had previously thought out-of-date. The older atheism seemed to be in trouble: like the older science, it was too clear and too neat.

Gradually her work took on a more personal flavour. It was as if she were not working on particles but on the meaning of everything. She found herself changed in her approach to thinking. She began to read poetry and even parts of the Bible. She had never been baptised, nor ever entered a church. But she knew something about religion through icons and art: after all it was the history of her country.

And then in the late 1980s everything began to change in Russia. Some of her fellow-scientists took *glasnost* in a surprising way and began to speak fairly openly about their religious views. Anna stayed silent, almost afraid of what she was hearing around her. But it caused another shaking of her previous certainties.

One day in the extraordinary year of 1990, Anna saw a procession in the streets of Moscow – a solemn event with singing and icons and incense. It would have been unimaginable even a few years ago, she thought, and something attracted her. She followed the crowd into the church. There she found herself surrounded by the extraordinary singing and was amazed by the richness of the ceremony. It seemed to uplift her as nothing had ever done. With one part of her she was aware that all this could be dismissed as mere emotion. Yet she also knew that it was putting her in touch with realities beyond the reach of reason.

She closed her eyes in that crowded church and sensed herself as part of something much bigger than herself. Millions of people had found wisdom here. Not the church building only but the Church as a community through the ages. Anna felt how vast it was, how it had endured so much trouble through the ages, even in Russia in her own lifetime. This vision had survived and had nourished so many people. What a joy to belong to something bigger than the self. It was as if her lonely search was not the whole story. This was a community of meaning larger than any individual. She opened her eyes and glimpsed the crucifix. It had all started from Christ. These were his people. This was what Church meant. Anna glanced at the hymn book held by her neighbour. He pointed to the place where they were. She joined in the singing . . .

Before going on to the next paragraph, it might be better to pause and think about the word 'church'. Does the very idea raise negative or positive responses, and why?

Try to list, even on paper, your image of Church and the reasons that underlie it. Make sure you try to look at both sides – the good and bad points. Why might we need a Church? Why do some people dismiss 'church religion'? You are not allowed beyond the asterisks until you do your homework!

* * *

Our guess is that the negatives were easier than the positives. Why is 'Church' a thorny subject? Because people have high expectations and are disappointed by the reality? Because many people have been hurt or let down by someone connected with 'Church'? Because it seems boring or out of date? Because it is too authoritarian or clerical? And so on. Here we are not going to debate the favourable and unfavourable features of Church life. Instead we are going to invite you to shift the discussion to deeper ground. Ultimately we want to look at the Church in the light of some passages of the New Testament. But before that we want to approach this topic from another angle.

Think of seeing somebody kneeling to pray. I remember being surprised once to see a Muslim at Kennedy Airport in New York, kneel in a corner of the departure lounge and regardless of the people around, he performed his duties, with bows and prostrations. After a while I began to admire him. It seemed a challenge to that very secular setting that he could have the courage to pray so publicly. I began to watch him not as a 'weirdo' (which I feared some of the other travellers were doing) but as someone doing something mysterious. It had its outer and visible side; it also had its inner and prayerful side. You cannot see prayer. You can see someone praying.

The Church is a bit like that. It has its rind and its core. At its core it exists to serve people on their road to God – and to do so in all sorts of ways. But so often we see only the rind, the outer reality. It too is real. But it is not the whole reality of church. Just as my attitude to that Muslim moved from outer to inner, so with my attitude to Church: don't judge it from outside only; enter into the core and try to see it at its best. This does not mean ignoring the failures or the scandals that are part of church life. But don't stay with that level alone if you want to appreciate its fullness. Just as you can only understand a person when you come to know them from within, as a friend, so you cannot really know the Church if you talk only of externals. If you are to appreciate the strangeness of Church, you have to allow for it being both very human and more than human.

When Jesus came to the region of Caesarea Philippi he put this question to his disciples, 'Who do people say the Son of Man is?' And they said, 'Some say he is John the Baptist, some Elijah, and others Jeremiah or one of the prophets'. 'But you,' he said 'who do you say I am?' Then Simon Peter spoke up, 'You are the Christ,' he said 'the Son of the living God'. Jesus replied, 'Simon son of Jonah, you are a happy man! Because it was not flesh and blood that revealed this to you but my Father in heaven. So I now say to you: You are Peter and on this rock I will build my Church. And the gates of the underworld can never hold out against it. I will give you the keys of the kingdom of heaven: whatever you bind on earth shall be considered bound in heaven; whatever you loose on earth shall be considered loosed in heaven.' Then he gave the disciples strict orders not to tell anyone that he was the Christ.

From that time Jesus began to make it clear to his disciples that he was destined to go to Jerusalem and suffer grievously at the hands of the elders and chief priests and scribes, to be put to death and to be raised up on the third day. Then, taking him aside, Peter started to remonstrate with him. 'Heaven preserve you, Lord;' he said 'this must not happen to you'. But he turned and said to Peter, 'Get behind me, Satan! You are an obstacle in my path, because the way you think is not God's way but man's.'

(Matthew 16:13–23)

If you had been around in Palestine when Jesus was preaching, would you have found it easy to believe that he was the Messiah? Most people, on reflection, would admit that it was hard to recognise him. Exactly the same difficulty arises over believing in the presence of God within the human reality that is the Church. It is the Church's nature to be this difficult crossroads. Allow for the problem – it will always arise when God enters human reality, whether it be in Christ himself, in the body that is the Church, or just in somebody praying. Look at these realities only from the outside and you will not do justice to their depth. A lot of talk about Church falls into that trap, and therefore stays on the surface of things.

When we read that famous passage, dealing with the foundation of the Church, it is consoling to find these two sides right there. There is Peter's great moment of faith – and notice how Jesus comments that this recognition by Peter has come from a level beyond the usual human way of judging things. Then follows the solemn mandate to become the foundation stone of the new community. But almost immediately Peter is seen to fall back into another and ordinary way of seeing things. His great moment is ruined, so to speak, when he argues with Jesus over going the way of the cross. Notice the powerful rebuke to him from Jesus, accusing him of thinking in a merely human fashion: Get behind me, Satan.

There is plenty to ponder here, especially about attitudes to Church. Within one conversation Peter fell from marvellous faith and from receiving an extraordinary mission as leader, into wanting God's ways to fit his way of thinking. To use our earlier distinction, Peter himself demonstrates the capacity to enter into the mystery of Christ and also to fail badly to reach up to the vision of Christ. And St Peter is to be the head of the Church!

Of all the apostles, Peter is the one whose personality is depicted in most detail in the gospels – energetic, impetuous, enthusiastic but also unsteady in his behaviour. It is as if they set out to highlight his failures, to expose the human weakness in the one who was to be the head of the new Church. It is Peter who sinks in the waves, Peter who does not want to have his feet washed, Peter who hears a command of love and shortly afterwards cuts off a servant's ear, Peter who brags that all the others may run away but he never will, yet who denies Christ three times. It is a picture of one man's frailty and how he changes into a man of courage after the resurrection and with the coming of the Spirit. It is also a powerful meditation on both the humanness and the grace of the Church as embodied in Peter.

This passage in Matthew is one of the rare uses of the word 'church' in the gospels, and notice that it is '*my* church'. That is a crucial little word. Jesus wants his vision of the Kingdom to be continued through a special community in history, and he identifies himself personally with that community or church. A later moment in the New Testament brings this out vividly:

Meanwhile Saul was still breathing threats to slaughter the Lord's disciples. He had gone to the high priest and asked for letters addressed to the synagogues in Damascus, that would authorise him to arrest and take to Jerusalem any followers of the Way, men or women, that he could find.

Suddenly, while he was travelling to Damascus and just before he reached the city, there came a light from heaven all around him. He fell to the ground, and then he heard a voice saying, 'Saul, Saul, why are you persecuting me?' 'Who are you, Lord?' he asked, and the voice answered, 'I am Jesus, and you are persecuting me. Get up now and go into the city, and you will be told what you have to do.'

(Acts 9:1–6)

This of course is St Paul's conversion experience on the road to Damascus. (It is interesting that there is no horse in the text but every artist has put one in!) Notice that once again Jesus uses 'me' with regard to the Church. Paul had never even seen Jesus in his life, as far as we know; but Paul's militant hostility to the new Christian community is identified here as an attack on Jesus himself. Once again we have an example of contrasting ways of seeing the Church. Previously Paul had seen this new group as a dangerous enemy to his religion. But from this moment on, he begins to see things with new eyes of faith. In fact, he will become *the* great thinker among the early Christians: it is Paul who later speaks of Christ as 'the head of the Church, which is his Body' (Ephesians 1:22).

In all these passages we find two key truths. Firstly, the Church only makes sense as intended by Christ to continue his own work in the world; secondly, I can never understand the Church properly from a purely human point of view.

In this light and as a help towards prayer, let us take a personal passage from St Paul himself:

. . . it is not ourselves that we are preaching, but Christ Jesus as the Lord, and ourselves as your servants for Jesus' sake. It is the same God that said, 'Let there be light shining out of darkness', who has shone in our minds to radiate the light of the knowledge of God's glory, the glory on the face of Christ.

We are only the earthenware jars that hold this treasure, to make it clear that such an overwhelming power comes from God and not from us.

(2 Corinthians 4:5–7)

The Church is only the servant of Christ's vision of the kingdom. But the Church is not the kingdom. In its human aspects the Church is like that clay vessel. As human reality, it will always be letting itself down and falling short of the Kingdom ideal. It will always be in need of renewal and purification. But the Church is more than its human side: it is promised the power of God and the presence of the Spirit.

Some months after her first encounter with the Church, Anna undertook a programme of preparation for baptism, the sacrament of saying yes to the way of Christ and of entering his community. She had come to the Church as a tourist or spectator, but gradually she came to know it as her spiritual home. Why? Not because it was a perfect institution in every way. Not because everyone who belonged to the Church was a saint. Not because she always liked what she found on a human level. But because this place was the home of God's truth. In spite of everything, it was the meeting place between people and God. Above all, it preserved the memory of Jesus for people – not just as a figure from past history but as a living presence. His memory was both sacred and subversive for Anna. It consoled her with God's love and it challenged her to learn another love in human reality. This, for Anna, was the core of the Church.

FOR REFLECTION AND PRAYER

Lord Jesus, you said this was 'your church'. This is hard to recognise at times. Most of the pressures around make me critical of what I see as the Church. You yourself were hard on things that were wrong in your religion, but you were faithful to its core. How can I reach reverence? Or a sense of mystery? Or an experience of church at its best?

Which part of Peter is winning in me? The part that sees you as Lord? Or the part that resists the struggle and sees things only in a human way?

Help me to recognise both voices in me. Help me to accept the earthen vessel in me and in your Church, but to reach for the deeper trust. Let me glimpse you in your Church, and then I will be seeing truly.

Growth in Prayer

NIALL WAS TAKING PART in the school retreat. He was sixteen-years-old, interested in faith, and bright at talking about it. In a session, with six others from the same class in school, the conversation got around to prayer. As he said later, most of the time before that 'even though we thought we knew each other fairly well, we talked mainly about football or girls or school, but never about anything like prayer'. The talk about prayer began tentatively, avoiding the personal. They wondered 'did God really hear prayers' or 'what's the use of praying?'. As the hour went on with questions and opinions about prayer, gradually each of them was admitting that he did pray. They stopped their 'headtalk' and got more into their experience of praying, saying things like 'I pray in the morning', or 'I just go into the garden and smoke a cigarette and talk to God', or 'I really ask God when I want something', or 'I used to say prayers I had been taught, but now I pray in my own words'. Another simply said, 'I think God is more like a friend and I talk to him like a friend'. Niall said, 'I never knew that other people my own age prayed.'

Now it happened that he was in a certain place praying, and when he had finished, one of his disciples said, 'Lord, teach us to pray, as John taught his disciples.' He said to them, 'When you pray, this is what to say:

Father, may your name be held holy,
your kingdom come;
give us each day our daily bread,
and forgive us our sins,
for we ourselves forgive each one who is in debt to us.
And do not put us to the test.

(Luke 11:1–4)

As Jesus taught his disciples to pray, so he teaches us; and one principal way he teaches us is through others. Apart from knowledge and encouragement about prayer, another effect of sharing our thoughts about prayer is that one person helps another to change in prayer. In describing a change in prayer at a time like bereavement, or illness, or marriage, someone may realise that prayer has changed them almost without their being aware of it. Something like this often happens in a conversation about prayer, such as this one between Maria and Paul:

MARIA: 'I prayed in fits and starts when my husband died . . . I asked God that I wouldn't be lonely . . . keep me safe, God, I prayed . . . worried about people breaking into the house . . . and I wouldn't be sick . . . God heard some of my prayers . . . not the lonely ones because I was awfully lonely . . . but he gave me peace . . . I felt peace inside all the heartbreak . . . like a gold colour inside a black one . . . '

PAUL: 'Now I can see something . . . I found it very hard to pray when Jimmy [Paul's son] died . . . so unfair . . . but God didn't kill him . . . now that you say it, I felt something like that . . . like the gold inside the black . . . O God, give me more of that . . . stop me blaming you and let me ask you for peace . . .'

Paul's prayer had changed him and was maturing, but he mightn't have noticed it if he hadn't heard Maria's story. Without the shared experience of another, change and development can go unnoticed.

Apart from change in prayer, there is also growth in

prayer, and questions about prayer can be times of growth. When you pray for something – with your heart and urgently – and don't get it, you may ask new questions about God and about prayer, like, 'Does God answer prayers at all?', or, 'Would God answer my prayers if I was a better person?'. You won't solve them on your own. See the change in Joe, a school-leaver, in his conversation with Mary, who was giving the school retreat:

JOE: I've been praying for a long time I would get my leaving certificate. I wanted to pass. And I failed. I felt really worked up with God . . . angry . . . annoyed.
MARY: Angry . . .
JOE: Yes, I wanted to get through. I thought God would give it to me. After all I gave up cigarettes for the intention.
MARY: So you felt cheated or let-down by God.
JOE: Yes.
MARY: Do you still feel the same?
JOE: Funny, it's not the same now . . . I realised I should have studied more and that God wasn't to blame.
MARY: No, Joe, prayer isn't magical.
JOE: But I got something else out of it . . .
MARY: Something else?
JOE: Yes . . . peace. I got a funny idea that I didn't need this exam to be happy. I had friends and they were great when I failed. I got to know my friends better when it all happened . . . and I had a peace inside me.
MARY: You seem glad you have that peace.
JOE: Yes. It's nearly better than the exam.

Joe has learned through his experience of let-down, anger and disappointment, and through talking about it with someone else that God had something else to give him. Maybe he knows the meaning of the phrase in the gospel: 'Ask and it will be given to you . . . if you then . . . know how to give your children what is good, how much more will the heavenly Father give the Holy Spirit to those who ask him!' (Luke 11:9–13). What Jesus promises to give in answer to prayer is the Holy Spirit, and 'good things to those who ask the Father' (Matthew 7:11).

This Holy Spirit is the gift of peace in trouble, compassion in weakness, 'the gold in the black', a sense of the love and presence of God which is always in life. Can we ask just for that, and leave the rest to God? He doesn't promise anything else. Is not the Holy Spirit the best gift of all?

Niall's group found confidence about praying. They knew that they weren't on their own in prayer, that people of their own age gave some time and effort to prayer, and had similar questions and problems. This is a relevant discovery in the late teens and early twenties; in trust and honesty they took steps to maturity in prayer.

After Paul's conversation with Maria, he was able to put words on his own experience. He also found that some of Jesus's words expressed his own experience. This is what we find when we share the gospel: it is a series of images and stories and exhortations coming out of a community's experience of Jesus and their beliefs about him. The evangelists are the mouthpieces and spokespeople of the early community, not just of their own experiences.

Growth in prayer doesn't happen in isolation. We learn to pray from others: most of us said our first prayers with the help of our parents. The first sign of the cross was traced on our foreheads and thus we learned how to make that simple prayer. We learn to interpret our experiences in the light of the gospel as in Joe's conversation with Mary. We help each other grow up in our relationship with God.

We learned to pray by praying with others, and by talking honestly about our experience of prayer: in the family or at school or with a group on retreat. Or we read about prayer, and saw our own insights mirrored in the writer's thoughts. Or we may find a prayer guide or spiritual director who helps us recognise the contours in our own map of prayer. Most of what we learn about prayer comes from others.

You don't learn to pray on your own, just as you don't grow in any aspect of Christian life on your own. Prayer is a co-operative effort within small groups, within the family and within the Church.

To learn to pray from and with others demands trust, as does any initiative of Christian growth. We trust our experience to the ears of others, sometimes to an experienced guide in prayer, and we trust that they can hear it. And we do this in the atmosphere of Jesus: 'Where two or three are gathered in my name, there I am in their midst.'

Contemporary aids to prayer include prayer-groups, spiritual direction and associations of 'faith-friends'. There are prayer groups of different kinds: charismatic prayer, quiet prayer or other forms of prayer. Some courses on prayer include a time of actually praying together followed by some teaching or input about the subject of prayer. Thus we grow in our attitude to prayer, in our questions about it and in our relationship with God. All of this happens as a result of working together with others.

A barrier to our growth in prayer can be that we don't talk about it to anyone and just give it up. Or we keep praying as we did when we were children and don't move on. Or we have an image of God which hasn't changed since childhood.

On a day's retreat, a woman called Mary said that her God had little time for the place where she lived – a very poor parish, with every social problem you could think of. Mary was separated from her husband and had three children by two fathers. She couldn't pray. But Josie, her neighbour, said that Jesus always loved the poor. 'If he came to .... (naming the parish), he'd set up house in our block of flats because he always went among the poor.'

Have you found that your view of God changed when you talked about it with someone? Our view or image of God changes in a community of prayer. Our image of God is the type of God we pray to; it is not just a picture of God, but may include that.

For example, one image of God is as a punishing God: a lady said to me after the death of her daughter, herself the mother of a young family, 'God must be punishing me for what I did wrong in the past, but I can't remember much he might punish me for.'

Or you might have a view of God which is all-divine, or all-human. Some have a harsh picture of God, the one always ready to catch you out, or the prescription-God who almost waves a magic wand or writes a pain-killing prescription to ease the burden of life; the expectation of this God is that all prayers will be immediately answered in the way I want them.

Many other images describe God in harsh, remote, childish or unreal ways which are untrue to the gospel.

God in the gospel of Jesus is always close, forgiving, on your side. In the words of St Augustine, God is 'loving you most when you love yourself least', calling you to be the person he sees you can become, inviting you into the following of Jesus.

In the case of Mary and Josie, there were two distinct images of God. For Mary, God would not be at home among the poor, and people like her. For Josie, God would go first to make his home among the poor.

Your image of God affects how you feel when you pray. If God is the all-seeing, always watching God, then you feel afraid; if God is the prescription God then you feel angry at not getting what you want; if God is an all-human God you miss his majesty and awesomeness, but if he is all-divine (as is more often the case) you never tell him how you feel, and he becomes more and more remote, looking on the world from a distance. But look at some of the Scriptures for how God describes himself: *Luke 15*: God searches for the person who is lost, waits

for the person who has strayed. He is joyful when a person returns or is found.
Luke 18:35–43: God wants to heal and help a person – he asks what the person is looking for. He is fully in touch with the person who is speaking to him.
John 15:9–17: God in Jesus calls himself our friend, and from the circle of Divine Love, calls us to love one another.

FOR REFLECTION

1. Who taught you to pray? Recall various people in your life who were God's teachers of prayer to you: your family, friends, teachers, prayer guides, retreat directors. Thank God for them: they have been teachers of prayer.
2. We know what Jesus taught his disciples. What were you taught? Can you recall times when someone helped you make a change in your prayer life? Or taught you different methods of prayer? Did this happen alone, or with others?
3. Have you ever been a help to someone in their life of prayer?
4. Of the different images of God given here, which do you think is most like the God of Revelation? Reflect whether any of them strike you as close to your image of God? Could you share on different images of God in your group, and see how your images may become more like what God says of himself?

PRAYER

Lord open my eyes for a true vision of what you are like,
open my ears to hear the love and call of your word,
open my heart to know your love;
open my hands to work with you in the service of others.

Make me truly grateful for who you are
and for your friendship-care of me all these years.

Be with me, Lord, and be with all
I hold dear in my heart this day,
now and forever.

Community in Action

PLACE: ROME.
TIME: Midday, Christmas Day, 1990.
SETTING: Church of Santa Maria in Trastevere (one of the oldest sites of Christian worship).
SCENE: The main aisle is full of tables, at which hundreds of people are eating.
CLIMAX: The simultaneous popping of thirty bottles of bubbly wine on steps of high altar.
REASON: To celebrate the tenth anniversary of this Christmas dinner for the poor.
BACKGROUND: About 5000 young Romans belonging to the lay community of St Egidio have a commitment to praying together and to serving the deprived.

Change the scene to a cold and ordinary Tuesday night in February. The same church. The pews are back in place. The time is 8.15 p.m. The church is completely dark, except for a spotlight on a bible high on the altar and twelve candles in front of an icon of Christ. Gradually young people enter, many carrying bags, as if coming from work or study. Nobody speaks. An air of recollection reigns. When a hundred or more have arrived, suddenly the place breaks into song – a powerful hymn in harmony. Someone goes up to light the large Easter candle; at the same moment the famous mosaics burst into brightness, showing Christ and Mary enthroned like a Byzantine Emperor and Empress. But there is a delicate touch – Christ has his arm around Mary's shoulder.

Evening prayer continues, sung in disciplined harmony. There is a short reading from the gospel: judge not and you will not be judged (Matthew 7:1). A young man, wrapped in a red scarf, gives a few reflections. 'We are in the middle of a war and we are told to forgive. Christ's road is different always. It is a road that did not begin with you and it will not end with you. It begins always from him. He gives us the power to be a community of care.'

Every single night this twenty-minute liturgy takes place in various churches in Rome. Every night young members of this San Egidio community gather to be strengthened by sharing the Word of God together. They come from ordinary lives. Even to visit the scene is to pick up the contagion of their commitment. A casual visitor will almost always be approached afterwards and welcomed. No attempt is made to rope you in, just to make you feel at home and answer any queries. On that Tuesday night Lucia and Carlo came across to the two of us and chatted for some fifteen minutes. They had been in the community for over ten years. It was their religious lifeline in that it helped them live their faith in this very secular city. 'It's hard to be a happy believer on your own', said Lucia, who gives three afternoons a week to being with the elderly poor.

PLACE: San Felix, Venezuela.
TIME: Evening, May 1987.
SETTING: A church with all the seats arranged in a big square in front of the altar.
SCENE: A man dressed in a white soutane sits near the altar and listens as one person after another stands up and tells the story of their faith and hope as a community.
CLIMAX: Eventually the man in white replies: 'I want you to know how marvellous it is for me to hear your story and your struggles as Christians. It will give joy to

this new job of mine to know you are there.' Applause breaks out.
REASON: A newly-appointed bishop is visiting a parish organised into many 'basic Christian communities'.
BACKGROUND: In Latin America the Church's option for the poor often takes the form of this 'from below' listening to lay communities of ordinary people.

Again change the scene to the ordinary community supports that make this special occasion possible. Take another ordinary Tuesday night in the same place. A group of about ten gathers at Fernanda's little house or hut. Because of the heat, they sit outside in the open air. Irene, the leader of the little community, is about fifty. Some people bring Bibles, but Irene cannot read, so when they begin with a passage from the gospel, she closes her eyes and listens deeply – as if harvesting every word carefully.

This evening, they have taken the Beatitudes:

Seeing the crowds, he went onto the mountain. And when he was seated his disciples came to him. Then he began to speak. This is what he taught them:

> How blessed are the poor in spirit:
> the kingdom of Heaven is theirs.
> Blessed are the gentle:
> they shall have the earth as inheritance.
> Blessed are those who mourn:
> they shall be comforted.
> Blessed are those
>   who hunger and thirst for uprightness:
> they shall have their fill.
> Blessed are the merciful:
> they shall have mercy shown them.
> Blessed are the pure in heart:
> they shall see God.
> Blessed are the peace-makers:

they shall be recognised
as children of God.
Blessed are those who are persecuted
in the cause of uprightness:
the kingdom of Heaven is theirs.

(Matthew 5:1–12)

After the reading everyone sits in silence. This week it is Maximo's turn to lead the reflection. He has already pondered these words of Jesus many times but particularly during the past week. What he says comes from listening to the Scriptures in the light of the poverty all around them.

'I think these promises are true here and now', he says, 'not just beyond the grave. I think Jesus is telling us how to be truly happy here. Because all these are his attitudes of heart, and we can enter into his vision through our own experience in this very *barrio*. Take just this last week: two children died of dysentery because of the water. We are asked both to enter the pain of that – to "mourn" – and yet to "hunger and thirst" for justice. We are asked to do that without violence – being "gentle" and "peacemaking" – even if our protests about the water are roughly handled by police or city authorities – "persecuted in the cause of right". Above all we are asked to be "poor in spirit" which means that our evil poverty of being wrongly deprived of our rights, can go hand in hand with a good poverty. Poverty of spirit to me means knowing our need to trust in God and to guard the vision of Jesus in all we try to do. If we act that way, we will be happy in our faith and in our community.'

These are just two real examples of community, but there are many others, and they answer many people's hunger. It seems that the impersonal society that is typical of modern life often leaves people isolated and unsatisfied. They would like to experience some trust and depth of relationship together. Perhaps many never manage to find what might help them, and yet especially in the last few decades, small communities have offered a key to growth in faith for many Christians around the world. It is as if the Church has rediscovered one of her ancient sources of strength. Because it was in a small community that it all began.

They remained faithful to the teaching of the apostles, to the brotherhood, to the breaking of bread and to the prayers.

And everyone was filled with awe; the apostles worked many signs and miracles.

And all who shared the faith owned everything in common; they sold their goods and possessions and distributed the proceeds among themselves according to what each one needed.

Each day, with one heart, they regularly went to the Temple but met in their houses for the breaking of bread; they shared their food gladly and generously; they praised God and were looked up to by everyone. Day by day the Lord added to their community those destined to be saved.

(Acts 2:42–7)

Let us try to flesh out this brief account, putting it into different words.

It is a story of a group of people gathered round a truth or doctrine, a vision of God protected from error by those who have a special ministry of guidance within the community.

It is a story of shared experience of life: some live together, or gather in one another's houses.

It is a story of freedom in material things, and of letting everyone have what they need. No wonder some have commented on this description as 'communism' in the best sense.

It is a story of companionship in worship and as a sacramental community: twice there is mention of 'breaking of bread', the code name for the Eucharist in the early Church.

It is a story of liberation and wonder: people are drawn by the 'signs' that are found (which need not be understood only as extraordinary healings but also as the miracle of love in practice).

It is a story of openness and reaching out to others: this community is growing, because whenever people glimpse the reality of the way, the truth and the life, they want to belong.

Think back on that description from the Acts of the Apostles, and ask how much of it was echoed – in changed circumstances of course – in those modern examples of community from Rome and from Latin America.

To ponder and to lead into prayer here is another scene from the gospels:

When he [Jesus] returned to Capernaum some time later, word went round that he was back; and so many people collected that there was no room left, even in front of the door. He was preaching the word to them when some people came bringing him a paralytic carried by four men, but as the crowd made it impossible to get the man to him, they stripped the roof over the place where Jesus was; and when they had made an opening, they lowered the stretcher on which the paralytic lay. Seeing their faith, Jesus said to the paralytic, 'My child, your sins are forgiven.'

(Mark 2:1–5)

Later in the scene, Jesus also heals the man's paralysis, but for our purposes we can pause there at the moment when Jesus offers the deeper and even surprising healing called forgiveness.

We have been thinking about community. In what way does that dimension of faith seem echoed in this scene? Not in the 'crowd' perhaps. At least here (as in the scene of Zacchaeus in Luke 19), they seem to be a barrier to getting to Jesus. But in two other little details we have a marvellous example of community. One of them is obvious – the four who take such trouble to carry their paralysed friend and get him into the presence of Jesus. You might miss the other example of community because it is expressed in one single word: 'seeing *their* faith'. There is no mention of the handicapped man's faith but only the faith of his helpers.

So they are carrying him in a double sense, one practical and one spiritual – through what they do for him and through how they believe in God.

FOR REFLECTION

1. On the basis of the scene with the paralysed man, try a fantasy exercise as a form of entry into prayer. First of all, imagine yourself as the handicapped person in that scene, someone unable to get to Jesus, indeed unable to do much for yourself at all. Spend some time getting in touch with feelings of helplessness and also feelings of longing to be understood in your weakness, to be forgiven, to be healed, to be able to walk . . .

   Next remember four people who have helped you in important ways – not necessarily all at the same time as in this scene. Pause on each of them, and on how they made a difference to you.
2. Returning to the scene, imagine those four people who have helped to carry you on a stretcher and even making the opening in the roof so that you can come into the presence of Jesus. Imagine yourself being lowered and the surprise of everyone in that crowded room.

Imagine a moment when Jesus looks at you and then looks up at your friends who are still, presumably, on the roof. 'Seeing *their* faith.' Think now of people who carried you spiritually, through the depth you glimpsed in them, even more than through anything practical they might have done for you. Who are these people in your life? Some of them may be the same, or they may be different from the four you thought of as carrying your stretcher. Again pause. Re-enter your memories. Be grateful before God for such people.

PRAYER

Find your own way of praying this – with words or images or silence.

Celebration of Companionship

BABETTE'S FEAST is probably best known as a film but it was originally a story by the Danish writer Karen Blixen. On screen it managed to communicate a most unusual blend of physical pleasure and of a gentle thawing out of people into community and forgiveness. Perhaps it was all the more unique in that the pleasure in question was eating!

The basic plot is as follows. In a remote village in Norway lived a visionary Deacon with his two beautiful daughters. He founded a religious community that survived after his death, but, by the time of the climax of this tale, the members had become old and rigid in their ways – and were far from warm to one another. By a series of coincidences, a refugee from the political upheavals in France arrives on the Deacon's daughters' doorstep one day and asks to be taken on as a cook. Her name is Babette and, as we learn later, she has been the most famous chef in the most expensive restaurant in Paris. Now with the two kindly sisters, she learns to cook plain food and to hide her past – until one day when she wins the lottery! As it happens, the centenary of the Deacon's birth is approaching and the aging community want to mark the event in their usual puritanical style. But Babette has other ideas. She persuades the sisters to allow her a free hand in preparing a special celebration dinner.

By another coincidence, General Loewenhielm comes to the dinner, to accompany his invalid mother. He was once a romantic admirer of Martina, one of the sisters, and he has never forgotten this love. Now he is a distinguished figure, who has travelled the world and who knows Paris in particular very well. Hence he, and he alone, is able to recognise the extraordinary dishes and the rare wines that Babette produces. The others enjoy them without realising how special they are, but the occasion becomes for them the equivalent of a religious experience. They talk of their memories of the Deacon, and gradually under the influence of the meal, they discover a new closeness with one another. People manage to acknowledge old grudges and to laugh them away. And all this is done with the greatest of delicacy, far beyond just alcoholic bonhomie.

At one point the General makes a speech, the most unusual one of his long career. He finds himself going beyond his accustomed manner and he surprises even himself with a religious interpretation of the meal. The gist of his speech is something like this:

> Such was our blindness that we believed that divine grace was over and done with . . . But a day comes when we open our eyes and see that in fact grace is infinite . . . What our lives once rejected is now being poured out on us in abundance: mercy and truth have met.

His speech tries to put words on this event of wonder. Later, the old members of the community surprise themselves by singing until after midnight and before parting for the night, they hold hands in a circular dance in the snow. 'The stars are much nearer', says one character symbolically.

This amazing evening ends with the sisters trying to thank Babette, as she sits exhausted in her chaotic kitchen. They learn that she has spent her entire winnings on this one meal for them but she insists that a great artist must always aim at the best that is possible. In the written version, the last words come from one of the sisters, who tells Babette that even in Paradise her genius will give joy to the angels!

Obviously there is more to *Babette's Feast* than can be captured in our summary here. But it is not unfair to see it as a deeply religious tale. Indeed, Blixen's text is studded with direct echoes of the Scriptures: it mentions the feast of Cana (John 2:1–12); it describes the joy of the meal in terms of becoming like little children (Matthew 18:3), or as the moment when their sins are washed away and become white as snow (Psalm 51:7). It could perhaps be said that the story is a variation on the gospel episode of the widow's mite (Mark 12:42). From another point of view it explores how religion can degenerate into a spiritless routine that stifles the heart, even while keeping the appearance of fidelity (see 2 Timothy 3:5). But most of all *Babette's Feast* is a celebration of *companionship* – and that very word in its Latin root means the sharing of bread. It shows people emerging from rigidity into gentleness, and from pretence of companionship into genuine companionship. It is a superb example of that change of attitude which the Old Testament describes as God taking away 'the heart of stone' and giving people 'a heart of flesh instead' (Ezekiel 36:26). In short it is an account of conversion to community, a conversion which comes about through companionship, through sharing bread together in a special way.

Now that very same day, two of them were on their way to a village called Emmaus, seven miles from Jerusalem, and they were talking together about all that had happened. And it happened that as they were talking together and discussing it, Jesus himself came up and walked by their side; but their eyes were prevented from recognising him. He said to them, 'What are all these things that you are discussing as you walk along?' They stopped, their faces downcast.

Then one of them, called Cleopas, answered him, 'You must be the only person staying in Jerusalem who does not know the things that have been happening there these last few days.' He asked, 'What things?' They answered, 'All about Jesus of Nazareth, who showed himself a prophet powerful in action and speech before God and the whole people; and how our chief priests and our leaders handed him over to be sentenced to death, and had him crucified. . . . '

. . . Then he said to them, 'You foolish men! So slow to believe all that the prophets have said! Was it not necessary that the Christ should suffer before entering into his glory?' Then, starting with Moses and going through all the prophets, he explained to them the passages throughout the scriptures that were about himself.

When they drew near to the village to which they were going, he made as if to go on; but they pressed him to stay with them saying, 'It is nearly evening, and the day is almost over.' So he went in to stay with them. Now while he was with them at table, he took the bread and said the blessing; then he broke it and handed it to them. And their eyes were opened and they recognised him; but he had vanished from their sight. Then they said to each other, 'Did not our hearts burn within us as he talked to us on the road and explained the scriptures to us?'

They set out that instant and returned to Jerusalem. There they found the Eleven assembled together with their companions, who said to them, 'The Lord has indeed risen and has appeared to Simon.' Then they told their story of what had happened on the road and how they had recognised him at the breaking of bread.

(Luke 24:13–20; 25–35)

This famous episode comes towards the end of Luke's gospel. It too is a story that starts in sadness and depression – a story of believers who have lost the salt of their faith, and are walking away in disillusionment. Strangely, like *Babette's Feast*, it tells of how they rediscover aliveness and hope through a stranger, of how they get in touch once more with a vision that seemed gone for good. It also finds its climax in a meal where the grace breaks in on them and where they recognise the presence of Christ with them all along. Indeed after this flash of insight, they find themselves wanting to return to the community that they had left in their disappointment. And so the story ends with them going back 'immediately' to the Church in Jerusalem.

There is so much that can be said about this rich gospel story. It can be seen as a series of steps along a road from doubt to commitment. The way in which it is told may even echo some of the stages of faith initiation in the early Church. The story falls into four acts, like a drama. The first is a ministry of friendship and of listening on the journey, akin to what is called pre-evangelisation; this lays the human foundation for grace to be received. The second is evangelisation proper, involving an encounter with the wisdom of the Scriptures. The third is a sacramental moment at the table, the eucharistic companionship which is *the* crowning moment for faith. Fourthly comes the re-entry into community with the journey back to Jerusalem.

The starting point for faith always lies in some human contact. In this case it means sharing the road and the questions, and it is significant that the two disciples walk *together* – first with one another and, even when they do not know it, with the Lord. At this stage they tell their story and Jesus listens. Indeed he encourages them to tell their version of *his* story even though they have, so to speak, the wrong end of the stick about everything. It is as if, like a good teacher, he starts from *their* deep experience. When that has been heard they are ripe for another kind of listening.

A second step brings us to evangelisation in the full

sense – to the threshold of realising the Good News as personal truth. Here it is fascinating to see that the source of light comes from the Scriptures, from the Old Testament of course. It seems that the focus of their Scripture reflection was the perennial question of *why suffering?* And Jesus must have drawn their attention to many passages of the Old Testament which evoke a Saviour who would suffer for the people. No doubt the so-called Servant Songs in Isaiah would be part of this greatest of bible lessons (see Isaiah 42:1–9; 49:1–6; 50:4–9; 52:13–53:12):

> His soul's anguish over
> he shall see the light and be content.
> By his sufferings shall my servant justify many,
> taking their faults on himself.
>
> (Isaiah 53:11)

But the conversation on the road was not a bible class in any narrowly academic sense: afterwards they will look back and realise that while he explained the Scriptures, their hearts were burning. In other words, this is a moment when they are profoundly touched by the words of the Bible as 'opened' to them by Jesus. The wavelength of the story changes from resistance to openness, from disappointment to hope, from their human horizon to a great mystery beyond them.

The third stage is the meal itself. But first comes a small but vital moment. Jesus seems to be going to leave them at a fork in the road and *they* take the initiative, inviting him to spend the evening with them. Faith is free. It is rooted in their decision to ask the Lord to come into their house. It is born of their newly awoken desire to go further with this Stranger. So at the end of this long journey, the meal is the moment of the Eucharist. They see Jesus taking the bread as he had done at the Last Supper, blessing and breaking it. It is as if that gesture revealed him to them finally and fully. It is their breakthrough moment into faith. They know who he is and that he is really risen. As in the story of Babette, this is the great moment of grace, the moment that renews their hurt hopes.

The final stage is that they need to communicate this good news to others, and with this spirit of urgency they return to the Church in Jerusalem. It is an eloquent example of how faith is not a matter of 'me' but of 'us'. It is not without its comic side either: when they arrive back to the community in Jerusalem, they discover that their great news of resurrection is already known there!

FOR REFLECTION

1. Read again Luke's story of the Emmaus journey. Take it slowly and pause on the details, trying to visualise them for yourself.
2. Look up some or all of the Scripture references given earlier in this section, especially the Servant Songs in Isaiah.
3. Now you are equipped to go further in making these passages personal and prayable. Recall times of disillusionment in your own life, moments when you walked away disappointed and let down. Did you have any friends on that road? Did anybody walk with you? Give this question at least three minutes.
4. Imagine that a Stranger joins you on that journey of hurt or darkness. Imagine yourself drawn to tell the Stranger your story. Put words to it. Try to voice the pain, even in silence.
5. Now listen to the one who has listened to you. This Stranger has a deeper vision to offer, a different light to cast on your darkness. Perhaps here you could take one of those Servant Songs and savour it slowly and personally. Let new desire be born in you – to know this Stranger more, to be touched by the wisdom that is there. So you ask the Stranger to your house.

6. Picture the gesture of the bread. Taking. Blessing. Giving. Let it speak to you quietly.

PRAYER

Lord Jesus, you gave of yourself totally – in the bread, on the cross, to your friends at the table, and to me.

I thank you for all the moments when I could recognise you. I thank you for all the companions who walk with me.

Take and receive my little life. Bless it with your companionship. Break me from my selfishness. And give me to others in everyday love.

So Many Witnesses

DEAR X AND Y,

I have never told you how you touched my life. Perhaps you would not believe it. Perhaps you have even forgotten the incidents that afterwards became even more important to me than when they happened. I have precious memories of times glimpsing goodness in you and in people like you. In retrospect these moments continued to have an impact on me.

I remember walking with you, X, and we were approached by a poor old woman. She wanted a cigarette. You smoked but had none left. A few minutes later as we were sitting in a café, you said you wanted to buy cigarettes and went off. There was a delay before you returned, and when you did, the packet you had bought was open and some cigarettes were gone. I noticed, said nothing, but afterwards the beauty of it hit me. So simple. So generous. It spoke to me many times since. It challenged me to be a little more like you.

I remember visiting you, Y, after you had lost your husband, and it was no ordinary loss. Not only were you a marvellous couple, but you had also lost two of your children in tragic circumstances a short time before. The third death was truly a cruel blow. I arrived knowing that I had no words to offer that could be worthy of your grief. I don't think you expected me to say much. So I just sat there and we remembered Louis. Then came the moment that touched me most. One of your small grandchildren fell and started to scream more in fright than in pain. Her mother and father were not able to calm her down. And you said, 'Bring her over to me.' She was hardly in your lap before she was completely quiet. And then you said something memorable to me. 'I know Louis is gone to another life. But to hold a grandchild is proof that life will continue here as well. Even more so than having one's own children.' It seemed wrong to comment. I left your house with that double image of you – in your sorrow able to console, and burdened with three close deaths, believing so much in life . . .

There is a moment in Dostoevsky's novel *The Brothers Karamazov* when the old monk, Father Zossima, is coming close to death. As his friends gather in his cell, he tells them of the book that he learned to read from as a child. It was about the holy men and women of the Bible, stories that touched the imagination of the young Zossima. And, he adds, 'What is Christ's word, without an example?'

The following great passage of the New Testament seems close to what Zossima was saying, and close also to the spirit of our two examples of X and Y. It comes towards the end of the letter to the Hebrews, when the writer looks back at famous men and women of faith in the Old Testament and wonders whether Christians would be able to persevere in faith, without the inspiration of others around them. These last pages of Hebrews read like a hymn in praise of community as a source of strength for believers forever.

Community in this sense does not mean just a group of people organised for some immediate purpose here and now. It is a much vaster vision. It includes the whole of the past, embracing all the wisdom of history, and all the struggles of people through the ages. The writer to the Hebrews goes still further: he wants to make an important contrast between the people of great faith before Christ and the even greater faith now open to those who know Jesus Christ. He comes to this powerful invitation:

With so many witnesses in a great cloud on every side of us, we too, then, should throw off everything that hinders us, especially the sin that clings so easily, and keep running steadily in the race we have started. Let us not lose sight of Jesus, who leads us in our faith and brings it to perfection: for the sake of the joy which was still in the future, he endured the cross, disregarding the shamefulness of it, and from now on has taken his place at the right of God's throne. Think of the way he stood such opposition from sinners and then you will not give up for want of courage.

(Hebrews 12:1–3)

Pause on each phrase and it will offer food for prayerful reflection. We are being called out of self-concern into self-giving. We are being encouraged to keep going even when the journey is tough. Most of all we are being invited to live with eyes fixed on Jesus and to discover in him a summary of the whole Christian adventure. He has already travelled the road ahead of us. He 'leads us' and brings us to fullness, slowly and through struggles, but surely. And what do we see in him? A tension of suffering and joy, of shame and victory, but at the core, a life of complete self-giving. 'No one can have greater love than to lay down his life for his friends' (John 15:12).

It is a turning point in the life of a Christian when he or she realises that the story of Jesus is echoed in his or her own life. In other words, each person is a unique story but one that re-writes the master-story of God in Jesus. Each story is a story of darkness and light, of a mixture of pain and joy. Jesus embraced that mixture, with faith, and came through the depths of darkness and of death. Having our 'eyes fixed' on him means learning to do the same in our unique and different journeys of faith.

Perhaps this seems too high or distant from our ordinary

selves. Come back then to the first phrase in the passage. 'With so many witnesses . . . on every side of us.' Jesus is the great witness, the key example of how to live and love. But there are others. And sometimes it is easier to be inspired by the living poetry of goodness in ordinary people.

Perhaps this is another way of seeing and saying why we need others as companions on our Christian road. On my own I do not wake up to what is possible. Without others I remain unchallenged in my hopes. Goodness is contagious, as Thomas Aquinas used to claim. Without the mirror of goodness in the lives of others, it is hard sometimes to imagine the flow of love that I too can live. I can continue with more courage on the long climb of sanctity when I am stimulated by the sheer goodness of the saints around me.

To talk of 'saints' in this way is in fact to use the language of the New Testament. Simply flick through the letters of St Paul and look at the openings: nearly always he begins with greetings 'to all the saints' in such a town or place. He means all the people who are trying to be 'faithful to Christ Jesus', as he says at the opening of Ephesians. And where does the word 'saint' come from? In fact, it is from the word for holy as applied to God. Think of the Latin of the Mass – *Sanctus, Sanctus, Sanctus.* At its simplest 'saints' are people who share something of God, and 'God is love' (1 John 4:16).

FOR REFLECTION

1. The real gift of others, then, is that they inspire us and keep us going in the long adventure of being a Christian. Think of the many ways in which people have influenced you for the better. You can glimpse something in somebody else, something shining and generous, even if it might seem small or hidden. In this way you glimpse something of God through another person. More than that, you glimpse something of God's hopes for you. Because what is possible

for someone else is possible for you too in your own way.

Try this exercise in imagination and let it lead into your own prayer. Think of people who would be your equivalent of X and Y. Recall moments that speak to you deeply, times when you caught sight of the goodness in somebody and were surprised into wonder, perhaps even pushed into new openness yourself. As with other suggestions in this book, beware of rushing this. To remember things superficially will not lead to prayer.

2. Read and savour slowly this promise of God from the Old Testament. It speaks of the plan of freedom for you:

> [what] I enjoin on you today is not beyond your strength or beyond your reach. It is not in heaven, so that you need to wonder, 'Who will go up to heaven for us and bring it down to us, so that we may hear it and keep it?' Nor is it beyond the seas, so that you need to wonder, 'Who will cross the seas for us and bring it back to us, so that we may hear it and keep it?' No, the Word is very near to you, it is in your mouth and in your heart.
>
> (Deuteronomy 30:11–14)

PRAYER

Lord, I thank you for my memories of those people who influenced me for the better. I think you were there in those moments that speak to me still. I think you are still speaking to me there. Those people are mirrors of you, are among your unknown saints. But they are known to me, and are calling me to my kind of sainthood.

Lord, sainthood is not a word I like using about myself. But yes, you have big hopes for me, and ones that are not beyond my reach. What moves me in others is in some way possible for me too – with your help, with your Spirit guiding.

Community in Eternity

AT THE GATHERING IN THE HOME after a funeral for a young mother who had died in a car accident, I met someone who was in tears for both this person and also for her own husband who had died in his early fifties, more than five years earlier. Her only consolation, she said, was 'that we'll meet again'. 'Tell me that's true, Father', she said over and over again through her tears.

They say that when you are dying, it is like entering into a tunnel. You resist at the beginning. But as you go into the tunnel, there is light at the end. A gentle light, becoming brighter, beckons you. People gone before you in death – your parents, family, friends, saints – welcome you from death into eternity. Gradually the brighter lights bring you peace and confidence and the presence of God. You go on, eager to go to meet the Lord.

A person wanted to know what heaven was like. 'A banquet', someone said. 'But I don't like food', she replied. 'Heavenly music', said another. 'But I can't sing.' 'Eternal rest.' 'But I love being active.' 'Drinking wine in the kingdom of heaven.' 'But I don't drink.' Then someone said, 'Heaven for me is a good long conversation with friends.' And that made sense to her. She was a person who found that time went by quickly in the company of good friends, with good honest conversation where the atmosphere was of friendship, openness, humour, trust and care. Now she could look forward to heaven.

These stories are indications that just as we can't live the Christian life alone, neither can we live eternally alone. Death is an entry into a new life of communion with God and community with others: of the communion of saints, the communion of our loved ones, of the family of God's people.

Our vision of eternity brings out our connectedness with all of humanity and indeed with all of creation: in the words of the hymn *Steadfast Love,* popular in the funeral service: 'May songs of the angels welcome you and guide you along your way, may the smiles of the martyrs greet your own, as darkness turns into day'.

We are welcomed into eternity by angels and saints, and by all of those we loved on earth. For we are connected on earth with those gone before us by our prayers and in Jesus Christ. We know when our loved ones die that love is not over, that they could not just disappear forever, that we still need to say things to them.

Possibly their full happiness in heaven depends on knowing that they are at peace with us. When someone asks me to say Mass for someone who has died, I often feel like asking them, 'Have you anything against this person still on your heart?' If so, the best gift they can send them is not only the Mass, but the Mass as a sign of their forgiveness of the other. Purgatory may mean as much being forgiven by others, including those of us still on earth, and forgiving them, as being forgiven by God. We enter heaven on a dawn-cloud of forgiveness.

On hearing this, one of those gathered round the table said to him, 'Blessed is anyone who will share the meal in the kingdom of God!' But he [Jesus] said to him, 'There was a man who gave a great banquet, and he invited a large number of people. When the time for the banquet came, he sent his servant to say to those who had been invited, "Come along: everything is ready now." But all alike started to make excuses. The first said, "I have bought a piece of land and must go and see it. Please accept my apologies." Another said, "I have bought five yoke of oxen and am on my way to try them out. Please accept my apologies." Yet another said, "I have just got married and so am unable to come."

The servant returned and reported this to his master. Then the householder, in a rage, said to his servant, "Go out quickly into the streets and the alleys of the town and bring in here the poor, the crippled, the blind and the lame." "Sir," said the servant, "your orders have been carried out and there is still room." Then the master said to his servant, "Go out into the open roads and the hedgerows and press people to come in, to make sure my house is full; because I tell you, not one of those who were invited shall have a taste of my banquet."'

(Luke 14:15–24)

The revelation of Jesus presents the after-life as community with God and each other: a banquet of all sorts of people with God. A privatised spirituality overemphasises the first of these realities. Heaven then is presented as 'me at rest with God, and maybe his blessed Mother'! It is a type of eternal friendship with God which takes place in the midst of other people, but with little reference to them. This is the interpretation of texts like 'I will go and prepare a place for you, and take you to myself' (John 14:2), when 'you' is taken in the singular rather than the plural. But what of the Scripture which presents heaven in images and pictures of community and togetherness?

Other images of the kingdom of heaven in the words of Jesus are predominantly those of community. Heaven is a gathering together of the good and the bad (Matthew

13:24–43); the net full of all kinds of fish (Matthew 13:47–50); five wise wedding attendants and five foolish (Matthew 25:1–13); a tree becoming large enough to shelter the birds (Matthew 13:31–2). The passport to this new community is very much how we treated our fellow humans on earth (Matthew 25:31–46). Does not this go with our notion of the community of heaven, and against an exclusively individualistic eternal rest which is too much part of our spirituality? True, the kingdom of heaven is also compared to the embellishing and the losing of one's own personal talents (Matthew 25:14–30), but Jesus' main images of the kingdom of Heaven involve the family of people.

Eternity is the goal of our 'interconnections'. Sometimes at a moment of personal reflection or prayer, or conversation which goes into the secret places of each person, we know with certainty that we are all part of each other, and this is heart-felt knowledge which may defy logic. The Irish poet, Brendan Kennelly, expresses this in his poem 'Connections':

> Self knows that self is not enough.
> The deepest well becomes exhausted.
> We could wander forever in a wood
> And through the trees not see a sign of love.
> Turn then where windy March blows golden hair
> (A drowning man will grasp the thinnest straw)
> And slowly in the ceremonious air
> Observe irrational redeeming law
>
> Connect the desert with the sun at noon
> Revealing open beaks, descending wings
> And bones that hint of spirits that are free.
> We open in a moment, love, and then
> Linked with the livingness of growing things
> Express the shell and comprehend the sea.

The connectedness we feel on earth is a glimpse of

deeper connectedness in heaven, and this is the life of relationship with God and with others. It is the life and the grace of God. Martin Buber, a Jewish philosopher, remarked, 'All real life is meeting'. The same sentiment is expressed in a poem of seventeenth-century English poet, John Donne, when he writes, 'No man is an island'.

A woman wrote after her father's burial: 'I felt that when we buried my father, I was glad he was going to the earth, for the earth is home for many thousands before him. We talk of death as "going to our ancestors", of "being gathered unto his ancestors".'

Our human body, dwelling-place of God, image of Jesus Christ, 'the first of many brothers', mingles with earth and dust, with trees and wood, and mingles too, even though we may be hesitant to admit it, with other bones and flesh, in the call home to God. We cannot be with God alone.

Just as you can't be a Christian on your own, neither will eternity be a solitary joy. A positive spirituality of eternity is that we will all be together, at our best. Together at last, when St Thomas More's prayer that 'we may meet merrily in heaven' is fulfilled, and we shall together enjoy the Lord, and each other.

FOR REFLECTION

1. Be grateful for the lives of everyone you know. Remember people, one by one, and be thankful for something about each of them, whether they are dead or alive. If you want to, thank God for them.
2. If all of God's people are called to eternity with God and each other, how does that affect my relationships right now, especially with those I need to forgive, think more kindly about, repair a relationship with? Pray for that grace to the Lord of eternity.
3. Ask God for the grace to think positively about death, and to offer your death to God now, for it is the gateway to eternal life.

PRAYER

Death is a gathering unto God, and a gathering unto the assembly of God's people, into the communion of all who have gone before us to God. It is a welcoming home into the everlasting circle of love. It is a gathering of all of life's love and hope, life's joys and sorrows, life's fulfilment and loneliness, into the love of God which embraces, welcomes, forgives and makes new every moment of human life. If we die with confidence in God's encircling love, with hope in Jesus' risen friendship and with joy in the warmth of the Holy Spirit, can we not live like this too? To accept death with faith as a peaceful friend is to accept all of life with hope as a journey with God.

> Lord, may those who have died in your peace,
> teach us to live in your peace.
> You are the creator of life and the lover of life.
> Your love for the life of each of us is forever.
> Give me always
> hope in your promise of eternal life
> love for all you will call to yourself
> and faith to believe in your promise
> all the days of my life.